ARCHIVES PROCEDURAL MANUAL

WASHINGTON UNIVERSITY

SCHOOL OF MEDICINE LIBRARY

Second Edition Revised

© Washington University School of Medicine Library, 1978
ISBN: 0-912260-08-4

PREFACE TO SECOND EDITION

The Washington University School of Medicine Library's <u>Archives Procedural</u> <u>Manual</u> was first published in 1973. It described in detail the operations of the Library's Archives Section. Although some of the procedures were specific to Washington University Medical School Library, most were of such a general nature that it was felt they could be applied to other archives. Therefore, the <u>Manual</u> was made available to other groups.

The second edition of the <u>Archives Procedural Manual</u> updates the first edition and describes current archives procedures at Washington University Medical School Library. The major addition to the Manual is a section on Oral History which describes the Library's Oral History Program and its Oral History Computer Index (See Appendix III). The section on rare books has been deleted because a Rare Book Librarian is now responsible for this collection. Flow charts 7-15 have been modified somewhat. Most other changes are minor.

Over 1200 copies of the first edition were sold, indicating that there was a need for information on day-to-day archival procedures. In addition, the Library is happy to note that since the publication of the Library's Manual, the Society of American Archivists and other archives have published their own manuals. As was noted in the first edition, it is the hope of this Library that after a series of such manuals are prepared, a general pattern will emerge to become a standard throughout the country.

The second edition of the Archives Procedural Manual is available to archivists and librarians, and their comments and suggestions are welcomed.

                                        Darryl Podoll
                                        Archivist

St. Louis, Missouri
August 14, 1978

PREFACE TO FIRST EDITION

Collections of archival materials in medical libraries in the United States have been growing rapidly, as greater realization of the importance of collecting and preserving the primary records of biomedicine spreads through the scientific community. The need to check facts, to determine the methods of science, and to study the history of ideas is now unquestioned. For that reason the Washington University School of Medicine Library began in 1961 to collect the papers and other memorabilia which illuminated the history of its school and the history of medicine, and it has used the archival collection in its experimentation with computers and with oral history programs.

An archival collection, however, cannot be effectively mined unless it is indexed and physically arranged in a way which will bring the documents and material needed to the enquirer easily and quickly. Beginning in 1964, therefore, the then Archivist, Mr. Walter Walker, prepared a manuscript manual to explain the ways in which both the records and the physical objects were handled in the Washington University School of Medicine Library. This manual has grown and been added to by the present Archivist, Mr. Darryl Podoll; and it seemed reasonable to make it available to other archivists who might be considering setting up their own systems. Although some of the directions and decisions refer to specific Washington University School of Medicine situations, most of them are of a general nature and ought to be useful to a larger group.

It is the hope of the Library that after a series of such manuals are prepared by many archival institutions, a general pattern might emerge to become a standard throughout the country. To that end, we request others who have produced similar works to send a copy to this Library.

Estelle Brodman, Ph.D.
Librarian and Professor of Medical History

St. Louis, Missouri
November 15, 1973

Library Manual A-i

Subject: Table of Contents.

Library Manual A-ii

Subject: Table of Contents (continued).

Library Manual A-iii

Subject: Table of Contents (continued).

Library Manual A-iv

Subject: Table of Contents(continued).

Library Manual A-v

Subject: Table of Contents: Forms.

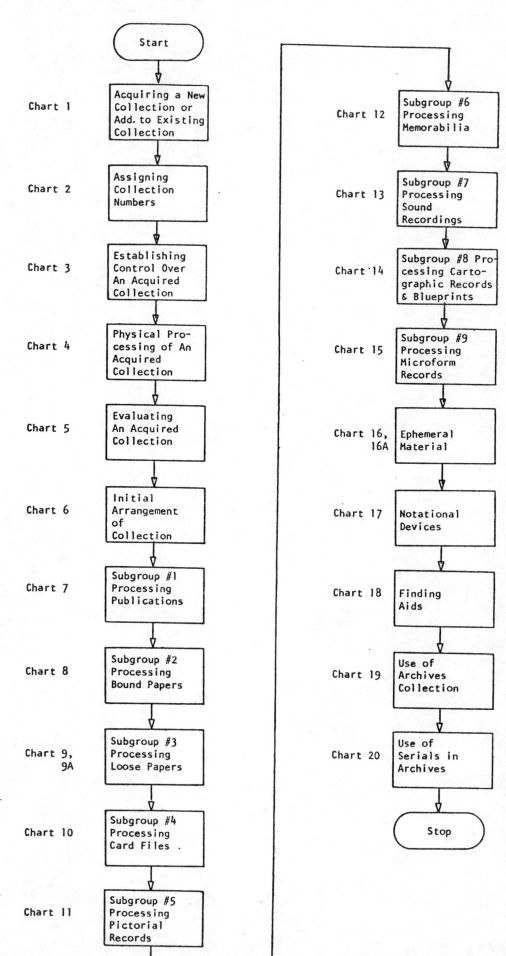

Library Manual A-1

Subject: Archives Collection.

A. Purpose.

The purpose of the Washington University School of Medicine Library Archives Collection is to collect, preserve, index and make available for use the following types of records for research in the history of medicine:

1. Private papers, correspondence files, notebooks, and other memorabilia of the members of the faculty and staff of the Washington University School of Medicine and the affiliated institutions of the Washington University Medical Center who have distinguished themselves for their scholarship, research, teaching and clinical contributions to the history of medicine.

2. Selected publications, reports, memoranda, correspondence, and other administrative records of departments and organizations in the Washington University Medical Center that have permanent value for the history of medicine.

3. Private papers of outstanding individuals in the history of medicine.

The responsibilities of the Archivist are set forth in the Program Memorandum. The objectives of the archival program are stated in the Program Structure.

B. Program Memorandum.

It is the responsibility of the Archivist, either alone or when the Librarian so designates, to identify and contact potential donors to the Archives Collection to persuade them to give their papers to the Library Archives. The Archivist will arrange for the transfer of the papers to the Library Archives where they will be stored under proper conditions. He will organize the papers in a logical manner and prepare finding aids. The papers will then be microfilmed in order to insure their permanent preservation. The Archivist will assist researchers in the use of the papers. He will conduct the oral history program of the Library Archives.

C. Program Structure.

The primary objectives of the Library Archives are:

1. to collect the papers of researchers and scientists who have made a significant contribution to medical science at the Washington University School of Medicine. This is accomplished by:

   a. being cognizant of important scientific research going on at the Washington University Medical Center.

   b. selecting those persons who have done the most outstanding scientific work.

   c. requesting the donation of the papers of these persons to the Library Archives.

(continued on next page)

Subject: Archives Collection (continued).

2. <u>to preserve</u> permanently these papers as a unique record of what these persons have accomplished. This is achieved by:

    a. storing the papers in a temperature controlled and humidity controlled environment.

    b. using acid-free document boxes and acid-free file folders.

    c. microfilming the papers and storing the master negative in a safe place.

3. <u>to index</u> the manuscript collections in progressively greater detail so that the manuscripts may be more easily used. This is done by:

    a. dividing the collection into subgroups, e.g., publications, bound papers, loose papers, card files, pictorial records, memorabilia, sound recordings, cartographic records and blueprints, and microform records.

    b. organizing each subgroup according to the principle of <u>provenance</u> ("that records should be arranged according to their origins in an organic body or an organic activity") and the principle of <u>original order</u>.

    c. inventorying the contents of each subgroup down to the file folder level.

4. <u>to assist</u> researchers in the use of the collections to facilitate their research. This is accomplished by:

    a. publicizing the availability of the archival resources.

    b. answering ready reference questions of a historical nature.

    c. guiding researchers in the use of the inventories.

    d. bringing out the documents requested by the researcher.

    e. assisting the researcher in the use of the documents (if necessary).

5. <u>to conduct</u> the oral history program of the Library Archives in order to:

    a. document the history of the Washington University School of Medicine and the Washington University Medical Center.

    b. describe the outstanding scientific achievements of Washington University School of Medicine faculty members.

    c. make the contents of the oral history interviews accessible to researchers through the Oral History Computer Index.

(continued on next page)

Library Manual A-3

Subject: Archives Collection (continued).

D. Procedural Theory.

    For the general principles of how to handle archival manuscript collections,
see Dr. Theodore R. Schellenberg's book, <u>The Management of Archives</u> (New York:
Columbia University Press, 1965), for the most authoritative work on this topic
to date.

This manual sheet supersedes all previous instruction sheets.

August 1, 1978

Library Manual A-4

Subject: Acquiring New Donations for the Archives Collection.

A. Responsibility for Acquiring New Collections.

The Archivist or the Librarian has the responsibility for contacting prospective donors and acquiring from them new manuscript material for the
Archives Collection.

B. Archives Collection Donation.

When a new collection is given to the Library, the Archives Collection
Donation form (see Number 80 following this sheet) is completed and signed
by both the donor and the Librarian. The primary purpose of this document
is to protect both the donor and the Library from any misunderstanding or
lawsuit arising from such a misunderstanding. Copy 2 of the signed document is placed in the Archives Collection Work Control File (see Library
Manual A- 13) for this collection and is available for instant retrieval
whenever needed.

This manual sheet supersedes all previous instruction sheets.

August 1, 1978

WASHINGTON UNIVERSITY

SCHOOL OF MEDICINE
ST. LOUIS, MISSOURI 63110

THE LIBRARY
4580 SCOTT AVENUE
(314) 367-6400 EXT. 3711
TWX 1-910-761-2165

STATEMENT OF GIFT

MANUSCRIPT COLLECTIONS

I, _____give the collected private papers (including

correspondence and other historical materials) of _____

("the collection") to the Washington University School of Medicine Library Archives,

subject to the following conditions:

1) The collection shall be available to scientists, historians and other
   qualified scholars who wish to use them for research purposes.

2) Although any portion of the collection may be copied or photocopied, it
   may be published only with the express written permission of the Librarian,
   Washington University School of Medicine Library, 4580 Scott Avenue, St.
   Louis, Missouri, 63110.

3) The Washington University School of Medicine Library Archives is authorized
   to dispose of any duplicate or unwanted material in the collection which it,
   according to its best judgment, determines to have no permanent value or
   historical interest.

4) Title to other papers that I may from time to time in the future give to
   the Washington University School of Medicine Library Archives for inclusion
   in the collection will pass to the Washington University School of Medicine
   Library Archives at the time the gifts are made, subject to the terms and
   conditions governing the collection.

Accepted: _____
                                                   Donor of Collection

_____   _____
Librarian - Washington University   Date
School of Medicine Library

_____
Date

STATEMENT OF GIFT

MANUSCRIPT COLLECTIONS

ALTERNATIVE PARAGRAPHS

With the exception that the entire collection shall at all times be available to the staff of the Library for administrative purposes, material designated as restricted by the donor shall be sealed for _____years.

With the exception that the entire collection shall at all times be available to the staff of the Library for administrative purposes, material designated as restricted by the donor shall be sealed until the death of _____.

The Washington University School of Medicine Library Archives is authorized to dispose of any duplicate or unwanted material in the collection which it, according to its best judgment, determines to have no permanent value or historical interest, provided that, before making any other disposition of such material, the Library Archives offers to return the material to me.

FLOW CHART 1

ACQUIRING A NEW COLLECTION OR ADDITION TO EXISTING COLLECTION

Library Manual A-7

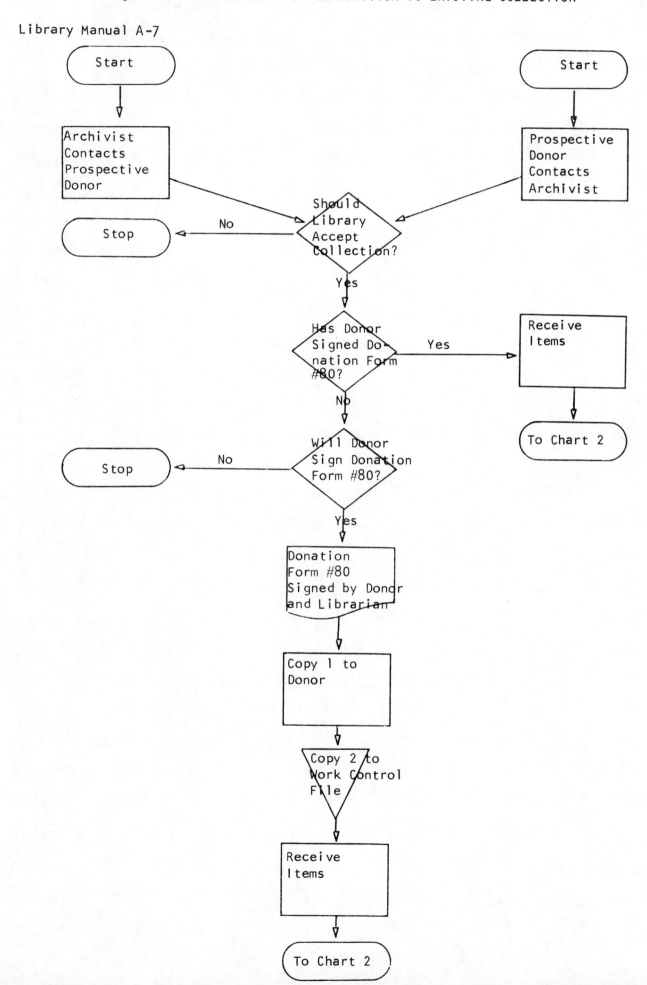

Library Manual A-8

Subject: Archives Collection Definitions.

The <u>Archives Collection</u> consists of all archival and manuscript records organized on a collective basis.

A.   Collections are the basic units for organizing archival and manuscript records and include:

    1.   <u>Record Groups</u> (RG) which are the departmental, administrative or other official records of the Washington University Medical Center given to our library because of their permanent value to the study of the history of medicine.

    2.   <u>Faculty Collections</u> (FC) which are the private papers, correspondence files, laboratory notebooks, and memorabilia of the most distinguished members of the faculty and research staff of the Washington University Medical Center.

    3.   <u>Private Collections</u> (PC) concerned with the history of medicine.

B.   <u>Subgroups</u> are the major subdivisions of collections and are usually determined by organization, function, or type of record; e.g., publications, papers, card files, pictorial records, etc.

C.   <u>Series</u> are bodies of similar records arranged in alphabetical, numerical, chronological, or other serial order; e.g., a general correspondence series arranged in alphabetical order by writer.

D.   <u>Filing Units</u> may be composed of single documents, single documents with enclosures and annexes, or assemblages of documents relating to some trans-action, person, case, or subject, depending upon the filing system used; e.g., dossiers, folders, pictures, etc.

E.   <u>Documents</u> are instruments, regardless of their physical characteristics, that contain information; e.g., letters, memoranda, minutes, etc.

This manual sheet supersedes all previous instruction sheets.

September 1, 1973

Library Manual A-9

Subject: Collection Numbers.

A. Upon receipt of a new collection the Archivist

   1. Determines whether the new collection is a record group, a faculty
       collection, or a private collection.

   2. Consults the Collection Number Sheet on the following page.

   3. Assigns the next available number in the particular type of collection
       chosen. For example, the Edmund V. Cowdry Collection was designated
       FC 8 because it was the eighth faculty collection added to the Archives
       Collection.

B. Upon receipt of additional items to an existing collection the Archivist

   1. Obtains collection number from Collection Number Sheet.

   2. Checks the existing collection's Archives Collection Work Control File.
       See Library Manual A-13 for a further explanation of this file.

   3. Determines the organizational status of the existing collection.

   4. Determines the availability and adequacy of finding aids for the exist-
       ing collection.

   5. Assigns only the collection number to additional items in the existing
       but unorganized collection.

   6. Assigns the complete notational designation (or portions thereof) to
       additional items in the existing organized collection. For a further
       discussion of notational devices, consult Library Manual A-45.

This manual sheet supersedes all previous instruction sheets.

October 1, 1969

Library Manual A-10

Subject: Collection Number Sheet.

This instruction sheet is a running tally list of all collections in the Archives Collection to date.

A.   Record Groups.   (RG).

1.   Washington University School of Medicine Collection.

2.   Washington University School of Medicine Library Collection.

3.   Washington University School of Medicine Department of Anatomy Collection.

4.   General Hospital 21 World War II Collection.

5.   Washington University Medical School and Associated Hospitals, Inc. Collection.   (Now Washington University Medical Center)

6.   Base Hospital 21 World War I Collection.

B.   Faculty Collections (FC).

1.   Joseph Erlanger Collection.

2.   Leo Loeb Collection.

3.   Evarts A. Graham Collection.

4.   Sherwood Moore Collection.

5.   Philip A. Shaffer Collection.

6.   Robert J. Terry Collection.

7.   Carl F. and Gerty T. Cori Collection.   (Collection not yet received.)

8.   Edmund V. Cowdry Collection.

9.   Martin Silberberg Memorial Fund Collection on Art and Medicine.

10.   Aaron J. Steele Collection.

11.   David E. Kennell Collection on St. Louis Doctors for Peace in Vietnam.

12.   Helen Tredway Graham Collection.

13.   Margaret G. Smith Collection.

14.   Borden S. Veeder Collection.

15.   Wendell G. Scott Collection.

16.   Carl V. Moore Collection.

(continued on next page)

Subject: Collection Number Sheet (continued).

17.   Bert Y. Glassberg Collection.

18.   Alfred Goldman Collection.

19.   Franklin E. Walton Collection.

20.   Valentina Suntzeff Collection.

21.   James L. O'Leary Collection.

22.   Hallowell Davis Collection.

23.   Jacques Bronfenbrenner Collection.

24.   Frank R. Bradley Collection.

25.

26.

27.

28.

29.

30.

C.   Private Collections (PC)

1.   William Beaumont Collection.

2.   Joseph Frank Mayes Collection.

3.   Henry L. Ettman Collection.

4.   Paul H. Stevenson Collection.

5.   Beckett Howorth Collection.

6.   James U. Scott Collection.

7.   Garrett Pipkin Collection.

8.   Max A. Goldstein Collection.

9.

10.

This manual sheet supersedes all previous instruction sheets.

August 1, 1978

FLOW CHART 2

ASSIGNING COLLECTION NUMBERS

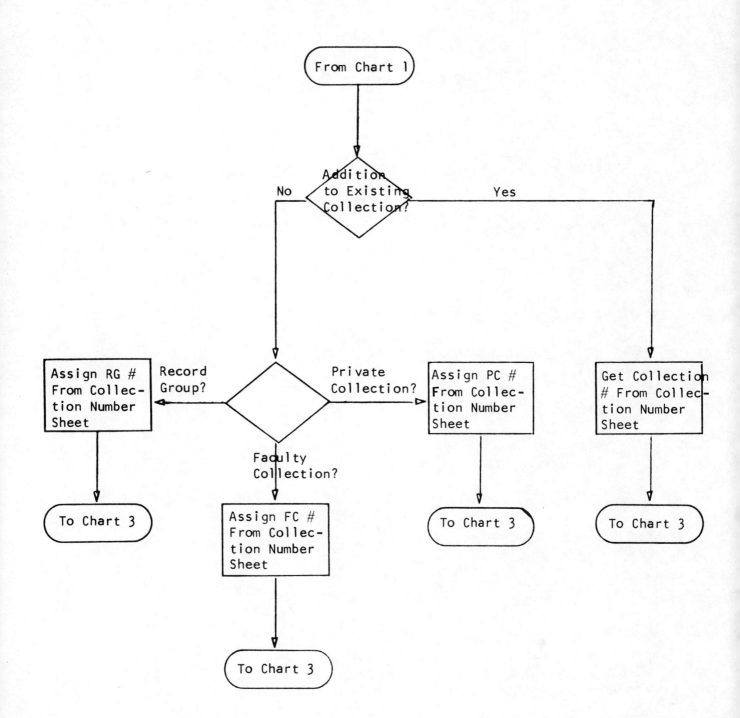

Library Manual A-13

Subject: Establishing Control Over an Acquired Collection.

When a new collection or additional parts of an existing collection are received by the Archivist, this information is promptly entered into the following records:

1. Receipt Register (see form Number 66 following this sheet).

   This is a chronological record briefly describing all material received by the Archivist, or transferred by him from one collection to another. For simplicity and convenience, collections of fifty documents or less should be itemized directly on the Receipt Register.

2. Donor Register (see form Number 68 following this sheet).

   This is an alphabetical record of all personal and corporate patrons who have contributed material to the Archives Collection.

3. Processing Checklist (see form Number 76 following this sheet).

   This is a summary description of the collection contents and an itemized statement of what has been and will be done to organize the collection on a permanent basis.

4. Archives Collection Work Control File.

   The processing checklist referred to above is placed in a folder, which is labelled by collection number and title, and then filed by that number in the Archives Collection Work Control File, a group of administrative folders containing the following information about each collection held by us:

   (a) Processing Checklist.

   (b) Biographical data concerning the person or institutional body for whom the collection is named.

   (c) Correspondence concerning the collection, especially letters from donors.

   (d) Notes, memoranda, and any other information of interest to the collection.

   (e) Information on each collection received between September 1964-December 1966 and recorded in the "Acquisition Register" and the "Disposition Register". For further information concerning these defunct files, please consult the Washington University School of Medicine Library, Annual Report, 1964/65, p. 62, "Registers".

This manual sheet supersedes all previous instruction sheets.

October 1, 1969

WASHINGTON UNIVERSITY
SCHOOL OF MEDICINE LIBRARY
ARCHIVES

RECEIPT REGISTER

DATE	REC. #	DESCRIPTION OF MATERIAL	DONOR	DISPOSITION	COLLECTION #

WASHINGTON UNIVERSITY
SCHOOL OF MEDICINE LIBRARY
ARCHIVES

DONOR REGISTER

DONOR (include name, address, occupation, and other pertinent data)

DATE   RECEIPT #   ANALYSIS #*   COLLECTION #

*(see Library Manual A-25, A-28 and A-44)

WASHINGTON UNIVERSITY
SCHOOL OF MEDICINE LIBRARY
ARCHIVES

PROCESSING CHECKLIST

Collection Title

Collection #   Notational Devices (If any)

Receipt Register   #   Date Entered

Brief Description of Material Received

RESTRICTIONS

Donor Register   Name Entered

                            Acknowledgement by Mail   Phone   Person

Fumigation   Date Completed

Other Treatment   Date Completed

Information on Folder Examination Sheets   Date Completed

Analysis Register   # (If any)

Microfilm   Yes   No   Date Completed

Inventory   Yes   No   Date Completed

Index   Yes   No   Date Completed

Remarks

FLOW CHART 3

ESTABLISHING CONTROL OVER AN ACQUIRED COLLECTION

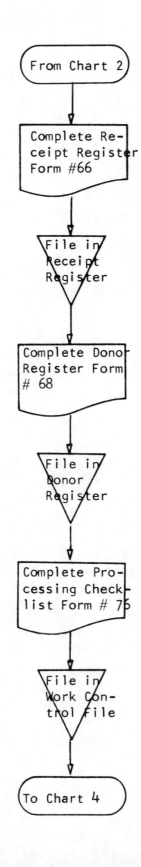

Library Manual A-18

Subject: Physical Processing of an Acquired Collection.

A. General Remarks.

Whenever possible, a small collection or an additional item to an existing collection will be simultaneously recorded, processed, and examined, as this procedure will give the Archivist a comprehensive understanding of the collection and will minimize needless duplication of effort. Initially, large collections should be recorded in general terms and described in progressively greater detail as time permits.

B. Specific Procedures.

1. All documents suspected of contamination by vermin and insects (especially silverfish) must be fumigated immediately by the Adroit Chemical Pest Control Co., 9457 Page Blvd., St. Louis, Missouri, (telephone 428-5363).

2. Documents requiring binding or special treatment should be separated from the collection and dealt with accordingly. Documents requiring deacidification should be sent to the W. J. Barrow Restoration Shops, Inc., State Library Building, Eleventh and Capitol Streets, Richmond, Virginia, 23219.

3. After deacidification important but fragile documents should be encapsulated between two sheets of plastic. Encapsulation supplies are available from TALAS, 104 Fifth Avenue, New York, New York, 10011.

4. All file folders should be replaced with acid free file folders available from the Hollinger Corporation, 3810 South Four Mile Run Drive, Arlington, Virginia, 22206.

5. All paperclips, pins, or similar devices should be replaced by stainless steel paper clips available from TALAS, 104 Fifth Avenue, New York, New York, 10011.

6. Pictorial records should be placed individually into acid-free insert sheets sold by the Millitex Corporation, 3305 North Sixth Street, Harrisburg, Pennsylvania, 17110.

7. For convenience in handling documents, all items 8-1/2" x 14" or less should be placed in the document boxes sold by the Hollinger Corporation. These boxes should be arranged in numerical order and the collection number, collection title, and the box number written on the box in pencil. The boxes should then be listed with notations as to which transfer container the records were removed from. The original order of the records should be retained when possible.

This manual sheet supersedes all previous instruction sheets.

August 1, 1978

PHYSICAL PROCESSING OF AN ACQUIRED COLLECTION

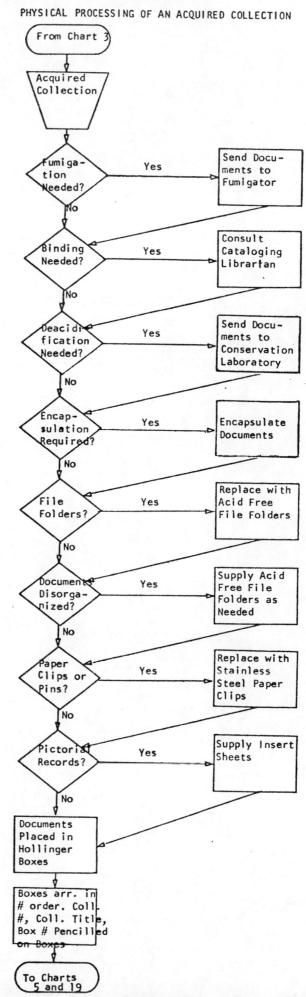

Library Manual A-20

Subject: Theory for Arranging an Acquired Collection.

A. Whenever feasible, bound and loose papers are arranged by the principle of
    <u>provenance</u> and the principle of original order because this:

    1. Serves to protect the integrity of records in the sense that their
        origins and the processes by which they came into existence are re-
        flected in their arrangement.

    2. Serves to make known the character and significance of the records.

    3. Provides the archivist with a workable and economical guide in arranging,
        describing, and servicing records in his custody. For an excellent dis-
        cussion of the principle of <u>provenance</u> and archival arrangement, consult
        the article by Dr. Oliver W. Holmes, "Archival Arrangement--Five Different
        Operations at Five Different Levels." <u>American Archivist</u> 27:21-41, 1964.

B. Most other subgroups are arranged according to type, size, or special char-
    acteristics.

C. Miscellaneous collections are arranged according to any scheme--alphabetical,
    chronological, or topical--that will facilitate their description and utility.

D. New additions to existing collections should usually be arranged in the order
    that they are received. For example, the original Evarts A. Graham Collection
    contained folders 1-1425, while the second receipt of folders continued with
    folders 1426-1568.

This manual sheet supersedes all previous manual sheets.

September 1, 1973

Library Manual A-21

Subject: Evaluating an Acquired Collection.

The acquired collection should be carefully analyzed and the following deter-
minations made:

1. The <u>provenance</u> and the original order of the collection should be determined.

2. A notation should be made of all missing documents and an attempt made to
    obtain the original documents or a copy of them.

3. The most suitable finding aids for the collection should be determined based
    on the collection's importance, size, physical condition, and anticipated usage.
    (See Library Manual A-48)

This manual sheet supersedes all previous instruction sheets.

September 1, 1973

FLOW CHART 5

EVALUATING AN ACQUIRED COLLECTION

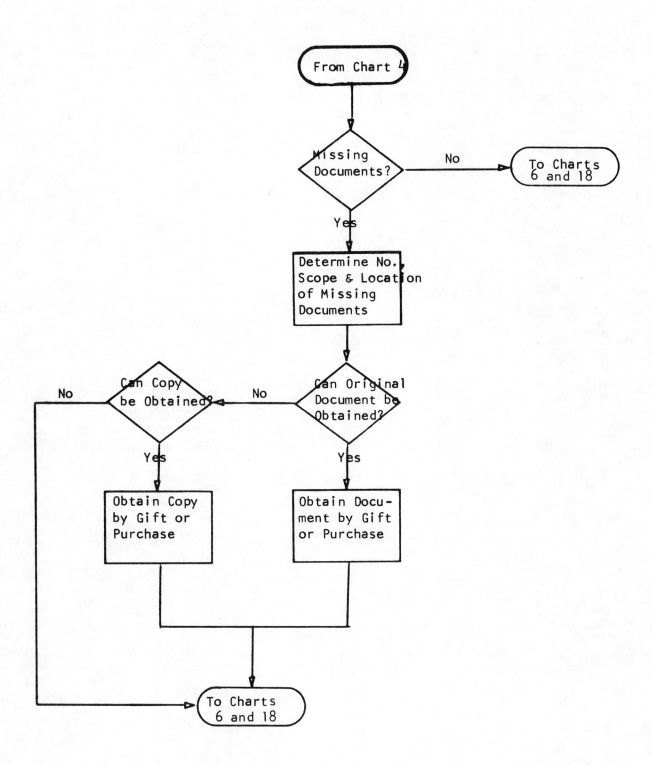

Library Manual A-23

Subject: Procedure for Arranging an Acquired Collection.

Whenever feasible, new records should be placed in the following subgroups:

Subgroup #

1. Publications--include serials, monographs, or loose items (such as news-
    paper clippings, brochures, or reports) that are not part of any manuscript
    folder.

2. Bound Papers--include accounting books, clinical registers, letter books,
    letter press books, ledgers, newspaper scrapbooks, notebooks, personal
    journals, and other bound manuscript volumes.

3. Loose Papers--include advertisements, brochures, invitations, letters (with
    any appendices and enclosures), manuscripts (published or unpublished drafts
    of articles, lectures, books, or other works), memoranda, minutes, news
    clippings, programs, reports, and other loose material. Pictorial records,
    memorabilia, sound recordings, cartographic records and blueprints, and
    microform records must be separated from the folders to which they refer and
    this information recorded on a Folder Examination Sheet (see form Number 77,
    Library Manual A-27).

4. Card Files--include invitations, lecture notes, research notes, subject files,
    or any other cards organized in some serial order.

5. Pictorial Records--include loose and framed pictures, portraits, illustrations,
    drawings, prints, motion picture film, and any other pictorial items. For
    microform records, see Subgroup #9.

6. Memorabilia--include awards, medals, trophies, pens, diplomas, academic cloth-
    ing, etc.

7. Sound Recordings--include glass and plastic records; disc, spool, and reel
    tapes; and other sound devices.

8. Cartographic Records and Blueprints--include atlases, blueprints, maps, or
    other cartographic records.

9. Microform Records--include microfilm rolls, cartridges, aperture cards,
    microcards, microfiche, and other microphotographic devices, plus all support-
    ing data, for example, microfilm targets. For pictorial records, see Subgroup
    #5.

This manual sheet supersedes all previous instruction sheets.

August 1, 1978

FLOW CHART 6

INITIAL ARRANGEMENT OF COLLECTION

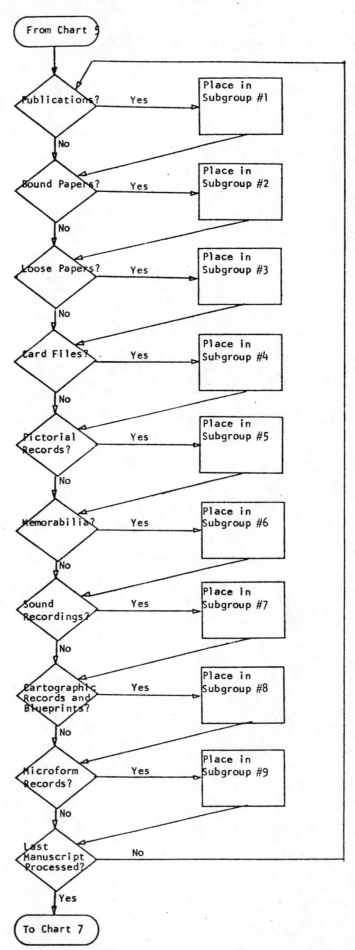

Library Manual A-25

Subject: Processing the Subgroups of an Acquired Collection.

Procedures:

1. Identify each individual item received.

2. Determine whether or not there is ephemeral material in the subgroup.
    (See Flow Chart 16, Library Manual A-43 for types of material considered
    ephemeral.)

    a. Itemize the list of material to be discarded on form Number 77, Folder
        Examination Sheet. File Copy 1 in the original filing unit and Copy
        2 in the collection's Work Control File. (See Flow Chart 16A, Library
        Manual A-44.)

    b. If the ephemerality of the material is in question, fill out form Num-
        ber 67, Analysis Sheet, and send it to the Librarian for her decision.
        After the decision is made, file form Number 67 in the collection's
        Work Control File (See Flow Chart 16A, Library Manual A-44.)

3. The provenance and the original order of the manuscripts will be maintained
    whenever possible. But, if after careful consideration, no logical order
    to the manuscripts can be found, the manuscripts may be arranged into a
    logical order. (See Flow Charts 7-15 for suggestions on the arrangement
    of the materials within a subgroup.)

4. If the collection is in a logical order, a descriptive list of the contents
    of the collection should be made.

5. If the collection is not in a logical order each individual item or unit
    should be described on a card or a slip of paper, in the format to be used
    in the Inventory. 8-1/2" x 11" card stock cut into three sections makes
    convenient sized cards. The cards can then be arranged in a logical order
    and the items put in that order.

6. Whenever there are pictorial records, memorabilia, sound recordings, carto-
    graphic records and blueprints or microform records to be transferred from
    the file folders in Subgroup #3 to their own subgroups, they should be
    listed individually on a Folder Examination Sheet, form Number 77, which
    attempts to furnish:

    a. a list of all pictorial material, memorabilia, sound recordings, carto-
        graphic records and blueprints or microform records removed from the
        folder or other filing unit.

    b. a determination as to the appropriate size of individual folders:
        folders containing over 1,000 documents should be physically divided.

    One copy of the Folder Examination Sheet should be left in the filing unit
    from which the material was removed. A second copy should be placed in the
    collection's Work Control File. (See Flow Charts 9, 9A, Library Manual
    A-31, A-32.)

(continued on next page)

Subject: Processing the Subgroups of an Acquired Collection (continued).

7. The Inventory is typed from the information furnished on the descriptive
    list or on the cards.

This manual sheet supersedes all previous instruction sheets.

August 1, 1978

WASHINGTON UNIVERSITY
SCHOOL OF MEDICINE LIBRARY
ARCHIVES

FOLDER EXAMINATION SHEET

Collection #   Receipt #

Folder   Other Filing Unit (Specify which type)   #

Title

Pictorial Records, Memorabilia, Sound Recordings, Cartographic Records and Blue-prints, or Microform Records transferred from this filing unit.

Ephemeral Material for Discard (Include multiple reprints, junk mail, or other items lacking permanent historical value in a medical archives collection.)

WASHINGTON UNIVERSITY
SCHOOL OF MEDICINE LIBRARY
ARCHIVES

ANALYSIS SHEET

DATE	ANALYSIS #	RECEIPT #	DONOR			
DESCRIPTION OF MATERIAL (Include item # record type, and dates covered)	QUANTITY (Lin./Cubic Feet)	ARCHIVIST'S RECOMMENDATION	LIBRARIAN'S DECISION	DISPOSITION		

FLOW CHART 7

SUBGROUP #1 PROCESSING PUBLICATIONS

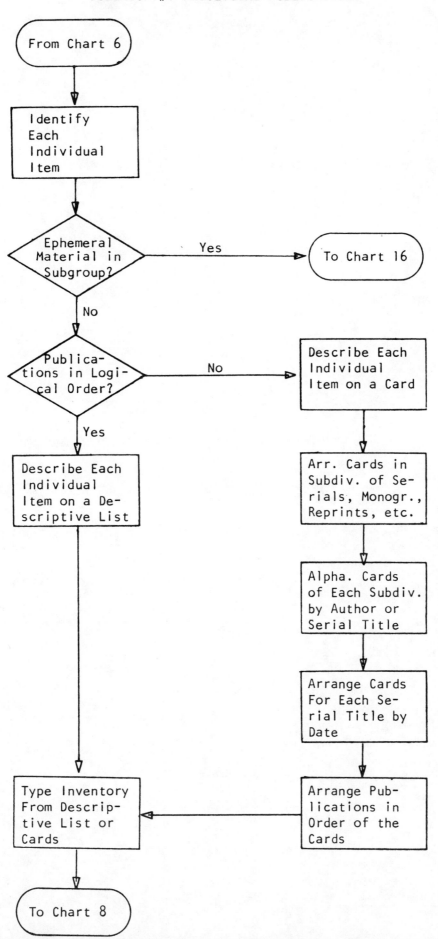

FLOW CHART 8

SUBGROUP #2 PROCESSING BOUND PAPERS

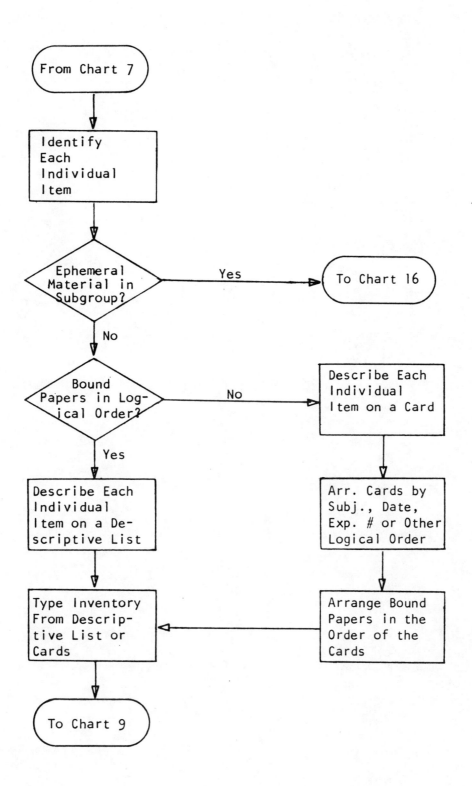

FLOW CHART 9

SUBGROUP #3 PROCESSING LOOSE PAPERS

From Chart 8

Identify
Each
Individual
Item

Ephemeral
Material in
Subgroup? — Yes → To Chart 16

No

Pictorial
Records in Filing
Unit? — Yes → Place in Subgroup #5 → Perform Routine 9A

No

Memorabilia
in Filing
Unit? — Yes → Place in Subgroup #6 → Perform Routine 9A

No

Sound Record-
ings in Filing
Unit? — Yes → Place in Subgroup #7 → Perform Routine 9A

No

Carto-
graphic Re-
cords & Blueprints
in Filing
Unit? — Yes → Place in Subgroup #8 → Perform Routine 9A

No

Microform
Records in Filing
Unit? — Yes → Place in Subgroup #9 → Perform Routine 9A

No

Loose
Papers in Logical
Order? — No → Describe Each Individual Item on a Card

Yes

Describe Each
Individual
Item on a De-
scriptive List

Arrange Cards
Alpha., Chron.
or Other
Logical Order

Type Inventory
From Descrip-
tive List or
Cards

Arrange Loose
Papers in the
Order of the
Cards

To Chart 10

FLOW CHART 9A

SUBGROUP #3 PROCESSING LOOSE PAPERS

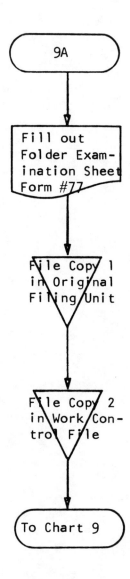

FLOW CHART 10

SUBGROUP #4 PROCESSING CARD FILES

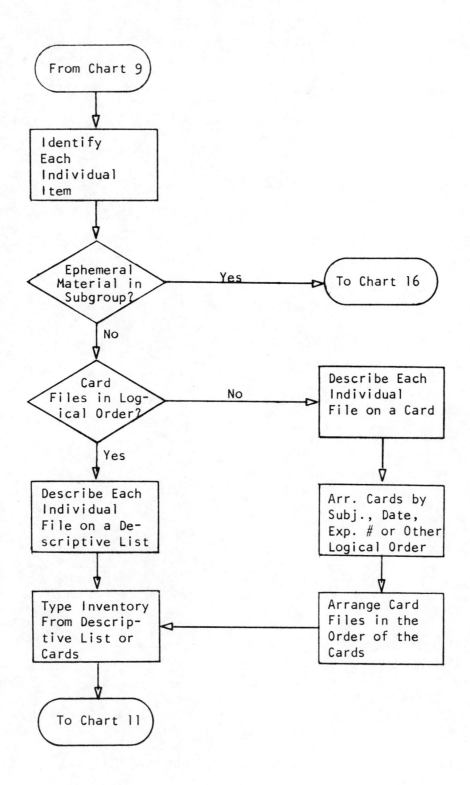

Library Manual A-34

Subject: Archives Picture Index.

A. The Archives Picture Index is a special record index of all pictorial records
(that is, Subgroup #5 records) in the Archives Collection, irrespective of
location. The comparatively high archival reference rate of pictorial records,
combined with their multiplicity of size, form, and difficulty of storage,
necessitated a special index for rapid recall and retrieval purposes. (See
form Number 78 which is reproduced on card stock for the Archives Picture
Index.)

B. Indexing instructions:

1. Verify picture information.
2. Type complete information on the blue index card (see form Number 78
following this sheet).
3. Indicate the name of the person or subject indexed as follows: first
name, middle initial, and last name. Also include birth and death dates
when known.
4. Indicate location of picture by class # unless otherwise noted.
5. Indicate all cross references on the back of the main entry card.
6. Write the following type of information on the back of each picture
indexed:

        Archives Collection
        RG 2/5/1/28
        Class 1
        Rec #68-57
        Description....

C. For storage purposes pictures have been divided into the following classes:
Within each class, pictures are stored by Collection Number. Pictorial
Records not belonging to any collection are stored by Receipt Register Number.

Class #	Type	Location	Sizes Inclusive (in inches)
1.	Loose	With Collection	8-1/2 x 14 max. (in Hollinger boxes)
2.	Framed	With Collection	9 x 14 max.
3.	Framed	Picture Box #1	9 x 14 x 24
4.	Framed	Picture Box #1	14 x 24 to 18 x 24
5.	Framed	Picture Box #2	18 x 24 to 23 x 34
6.	Loose	Map Case	9 x 14 to 14 x 24
7.	Loose	Map Case	14 x 24 to 18 x 24
8.	Loose	Map Case	18 x 24 to 23 x 34
9.	Loose	Picture Box #3	Over 23 x 34
10.	Framed	Picture Box #3	Over 23 x 34

The Alphabetical Picture File of Physicians and Scientists in Record Group 2
(Washington University School of Medicine Library Collection) is equivalent
to Class 1 above.

D. Although negatives, transparencies, lantern slides, and other pictorial
records require special storage treatment, they will be indexed similar

(continued on next page)

Subject: Archives Picture Index (continued).

to pictures and photographs. Groups of Pictorial Records on the same subject may be indexed on the same card.

E. Picture Inventory.

For selected pictures outside the Library but still within the Washington University Medical Center, a yellow 3" x 5" inventory card (see form Number 79 which is reproduced on card stock for the Archives Picture Index), similar to the blue index card is interfiled with it in the Archives Picture Index so that faculty portraits in particular may be quickly retrieved when needed.

This manual sheet supersedes all previous instruction sheets.

August 1, 1978

WASHINGTON UNIVERSITY SCHOOL OF MEDICINE LIBRARY
ST. LOUIS, MISSOURI 63110

ARCHIVES PICTURE INDEX

Subject:

Date made: size in inches:
Medium:
Artist:
Condition:
Where kept:
Collection #
Receipt #
Notes:

Date indexed:

WASHINGTON UNIVERSITY SCHOOL OF MEDICINE LIBRARY
ST. LOUIS, MISSOURI 63110

ARCHIVES PICTURE INDEX

Subject:

Date made: size in inches:
Medium:
Artist:
Condition:
Where kept:
Collection #
Receipt #
Notes:

Date indexed:

WASHINGTON UNIVERSITY SCHOOL OF MEDICINE LIBRARY
ST. LOUIS, MISSOURI 63110

ARCHIVES PICTURE INDEX

Subject:

Date made: Size in inches:
Medium:
Artist:
Condition:
Where kept:
Collection #
Receipt #
Notes:

Date indexed:

WASHINGTON UNIVERSITY SCHOOL OF MEDICINE
ST. LOUIS, MISSOURI 63110

PICTURE INVENTORY

Subject:

Date made: size in inches:
Medium:
Artist:
Condition:
Where kept:
Notes:

Date reported to Inventory

PLEASE RETURN TO LIBRARY

WASHINGTON UNIVERSITY SCHOOL OF MEDICINE
ST. LOUIS, MISSOURI 63110

PICTURE INVENTORY

Subject:

Date made: size in inches:
Medium:
Artist:
Condition:
Where kept:
Notes:

Date reported to Inventory

PLEASE RETURN TO LIBRARY

WASHINGTON UNIVERSITY SCHOOL OF MEDICINE
ST. LOUIS, MISSOURI 63110

PICTURE INVENTORY

Subject:

Date made: size in inches:
Medium:
Artist:
Condition:
Where kept:
Notes:

Date reported to Inventory

PLEASE RETURN TO LIBRARY

FLOW CHART 11

SUBGROUP #5 PROCESSING PICTORIAL RECORDS

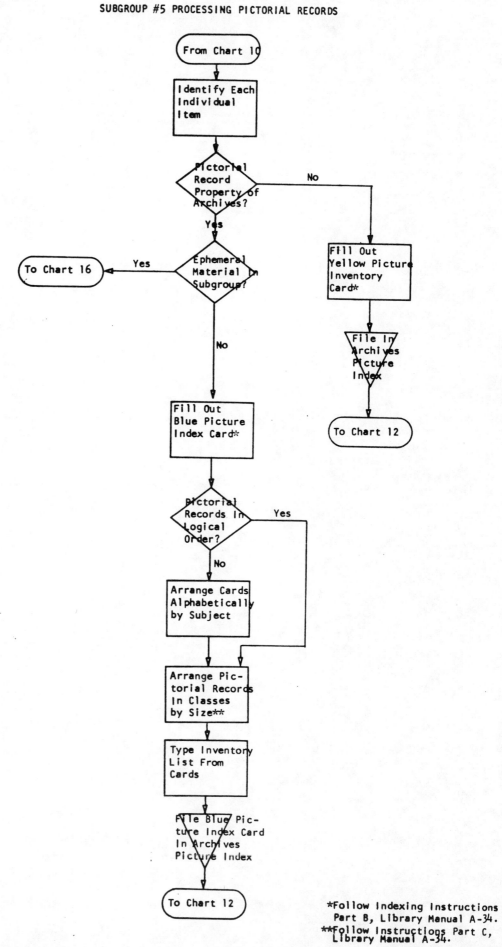

*Follow Indexing Instructions
Part B, Library Manual A-34.
**Follow Instructions Part C,
Library Manual A-34.

FLOW CHART 12

SUBGROUP #6 PROCESSING MEMORABILIA

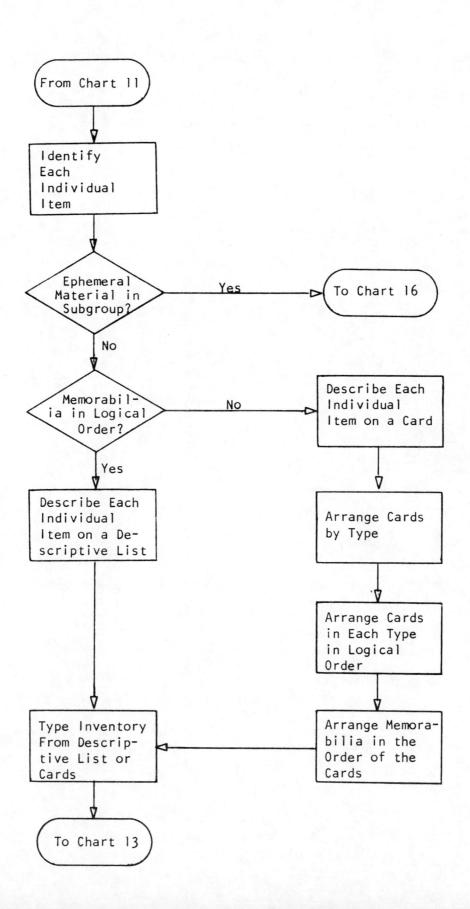

FLOW CHART 13

SUBGROUP #7 PROCESSING SOUND RECORDINGS

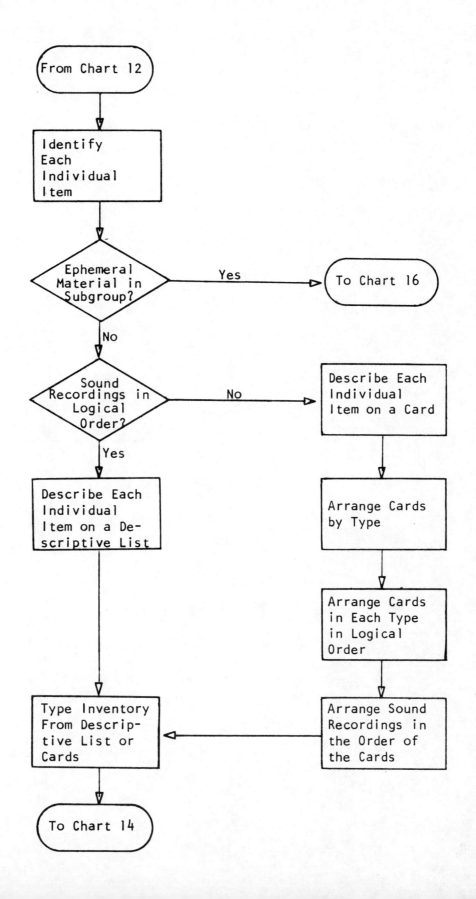

From Chart 12

Identify
Each
Individual
Item

Ephemeral
Material in
Subgroup?

Yes

To Chart 16

No

Sound
Recordings in
Logical
Order?

No

Describe Each
Individual
Item on a Card

Yes

Describe Each
Individual
Item on a De-
scriptive List

Arrange Cards
by Type

Arrange Cards
in Each Type
in Logical
Order

Type Inventory
From Descrip-
tive List or
Cards

Arrange Sound
Recordings in
the Order of
the Cards

To Chart 14

FLOW CHART 14

SUBGROUP #8 PROCESSING CARTOGRAPHIC RECORDS AND BLUEPRINTS

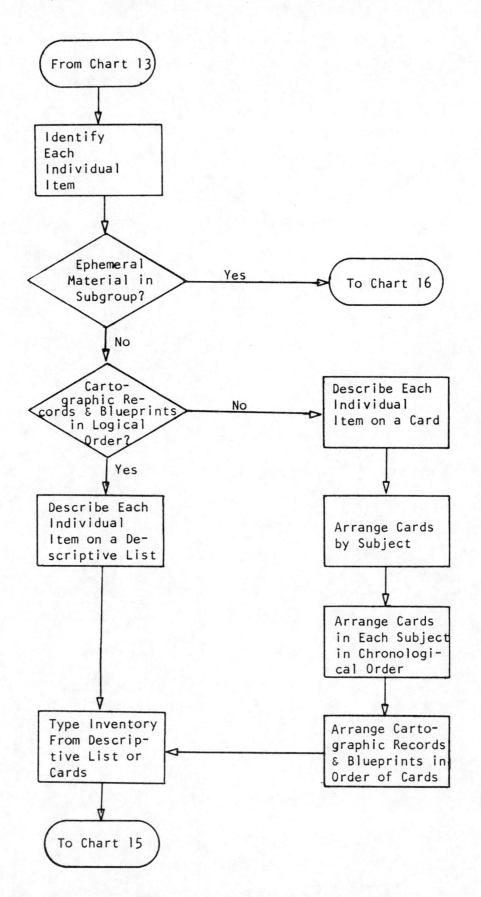

FLOW CHART 15

SUBGROUP #9 PROCESSING MICROFORM RECORDS

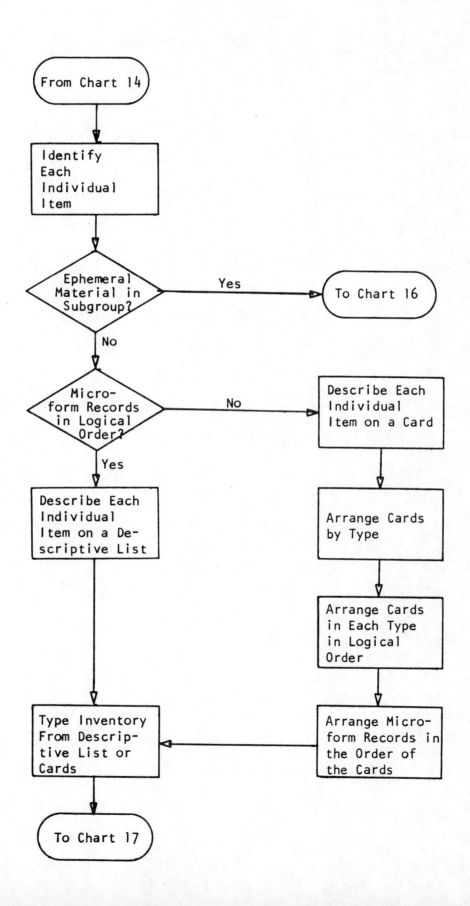

FLOW CHART 16

EPHEMERAL MATERIAL

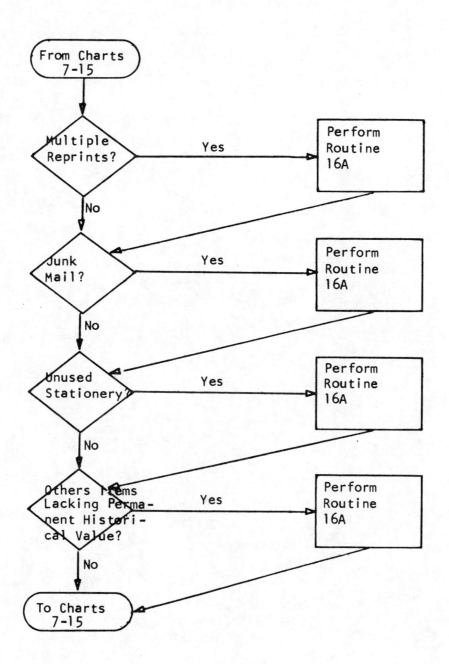

FLOW CHART 16A

EPHEMERAL MATERIAL

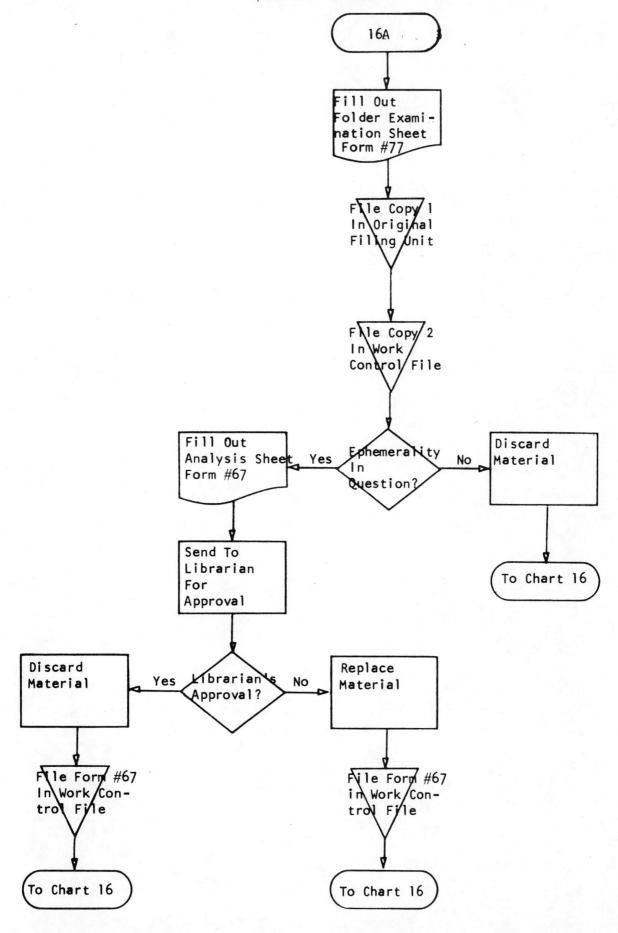

Library Manual A-45

Subject: Notational Devices.

A. Following the organization of a new Faculty Collection or Private Collection notational devices are assigned each filing unit, (and each document if the collection is to be indexed), composed of letters and numbers which serve as an archival shorthand for location and reference purposes. For example, FC3/3/1/1 stands for:

   Faculty Collection #3   Evarts A. Graham Collection
   Subgroup #3   Loose Papers
   Series #1   General Correspondence, 1919-1957
   Folder #1   A-Ad

B. For Record Group Collections (e.g. Washington University School of Medicine) Form Number 75 should be used. This Form provides for the addition of new records to the Record Group Inventory as they are given to the Library Archives. For example, RG 1/14/1 stands for:

   Record Group #1   Washington University School of Medicine
   Record Series #14   Student Fraternities
   Record Subseries #1   Nu Sigma Nu

C. Notational devices should be clearly displayed on:

1. All filing units or their containers, depending upon the type of record concerned.

2. All finding aids, such as inventories and indexes.

This manual sheet supersedes all previous instruction sheets.

August 1, 1978

WASHINGTON UNIVERSITY
SCHOOL OF MEDICINE LIBRARY
ARCHIVES

ARCHIVAL MATERIAL

RECORD GROUP #_____   TITLE: _____

RECORD SERIES # _____   TITLE: _____

RECORD SUBSERIES # _____   TITLE: _____

SUBMITTED BY: _____ POSITION: _____

DATE: _____

FLOW CHART 17

NOTATIONAL DEVICES*

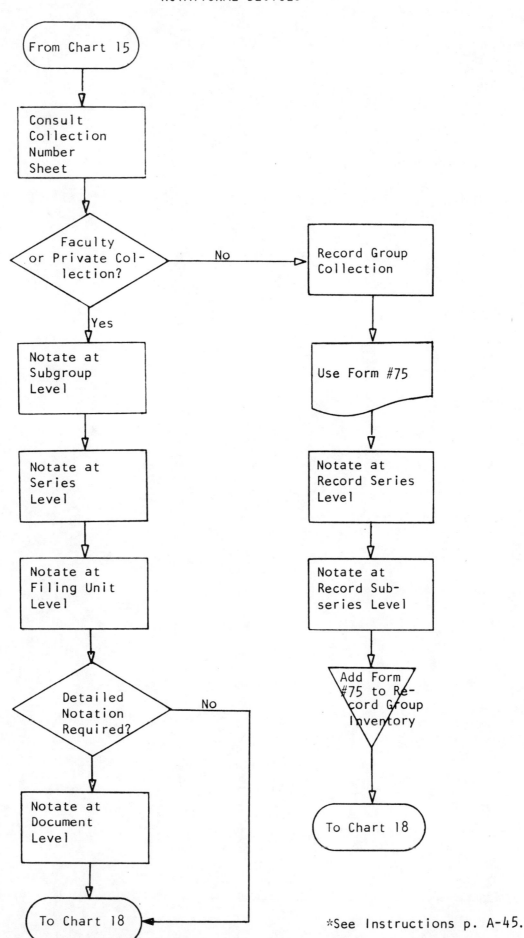

From Chart 15

Consult Collection Number Sheet

Faculty or Private Collection?

No → Record Group Collection

Yes

Notate at Subgroup Level

Notate at Series Level

Notate at Filing Unit Level

Detailed Notation Required?   No

Notate at Document Level

To Chart 18

Use Form #75

Notate at Record Series Level

Notate at Record Sub-series Level

Add Form #75 to Record Group Inventory

To Chart 18

*See Instructions p. A-45.

Library Manual A-48

Subject: Finding Aids.

A. Theory.

Acquired collections should be described:

1. Singly and collectively.

2. In a manner that will best facilitate their use.

3. In progressively greater detail.

B. Preliminary Descriptions.

1. The Collection Register is an initial finding aid for all Archives Collection holdings. (Between September 1964 and December 1966 it was known as the Description Register). Individual collections are described in summary fashion as indicated on form Number 69 following this instruction sheet.

2. The National Union Catalog of Manuscript Collections is a Library of Congress publication that attempts to index manuscript holdings in libraries, museums, archives, and other repositories throughout the United States. Therefore, a new collection should be promptly reported on the NUCMC data sheet available from NUCMC and mailed to the Descriptive Cataloging Division--Manuscripts Section, Library of Congress, Washington, D. C. 20025.

C. Permanent Descriptions.

1. An Inventory is a permanent finding aid that comprehensively describes a collection and is especially useful for large, complex collections with low rates of usage. An Inventory generally includes:

(a) An introduction discussing the provenance and character of the collection as well as access to it.

(b) A biographical sketch of the individual or a description of the agency which generated the records.

(c) A table of contents.

(d) A detailed listing of entries.

2. Microfilm is a photographic record on a reduced scale (16 mm or 35mm) of printed or other graphic matter. It is the policy of the Medical Library Archives to microfilm all collections as soon as their organization is completed. Since the Library has purchased an Eastman Kodak, Recordak Micro-File Microfilm Camera, Model MRD-2, all microfilming will be done in-house. For more detailed microfilm procedures consult Library Manual Appendix I.

(continued on next page)

Subject: Finding Aids (continued).

3. A <u>Computer Index</u> is an alphabetical or chronological list of specific names, dates, places, subjects, or other items which gives the notational device for locating each item in a collection. Its speedy access to individual documents makes it extremely useful for small, important collections with a high reference rate. Computer indexes have been made for the William Beaumont Collection (Private Collection 1) and the Oral History Interviews (See Library Manual A-68, A-69, and Appendix III).

4. The <u>Archives Picture Index</u> is a special record index of all pictorial records in the Archives Collection. For further details, see Library Manual A-34.

This manual sheet supersedes all previous instruction sheets.

August 1, 1978

WASHINGTON UNIVERSITY
SCHOOL OF MEDICINE LIBRARY
ARCHIVES

Library Manual A-50

COLLECTION REGISTER

Collection #   Receipt #   Analysis #

Name of Collection

Name of Producer

Place of Production

Kind of Producer

Record Type Including
    Distinctive Characteristics

Form of Reproduction

Dates of Records

Quantity

Name of State or Region Concerned

Subjects Covered

___Administration of Medical School   ___Pathology
___Administration of Hospitals   ___Pediatrics
___Anatomy and Neurobiology   ___Pharmacology
___Anesthesiology   ___Physiology and Biophysics
___Biological Chemistry   ___Preventive Medicine and Public Health
___Genetics   ___Psychiatry
___Medicine   ___Radiology
___Microbiology and Immunology   ___Surgery
___Neurology and Neurological Surgery   ___Other_____
___Obstetrics and Gynecology   _____
___Opthalmology   _____
___Otolaryngology   _____

Chronological Periods Covered

___Pre 1500   ___1821-1840   ___1921-1940
___1501-1600   ___1841-1860   ___1941-1950
___1601-1700   ___1861-1880   ___1951-1960
___1701-1800   ___1881-1900   ___1961-1970
___1801-1820   ___1901-1920   ___1971-1980

Include in a Descriptive Paragraph

Content of Collection
Receipt and Provisions for Use of Collection
Bibliographical Information Concerning the Collection

FLOW CHART 18

FINDING AIDS

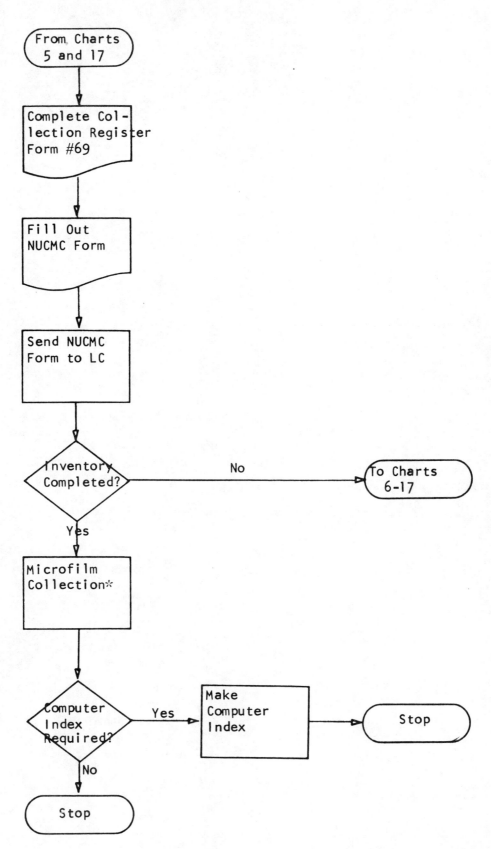

From Charts
5 and 17

Complete Col-
lection Register
Form #69

Fill Out
NUCMC Form

Send NUCMC
Form to LC

Inventory
Completed? — No → To Charts
6-17

Yes

Microfilm
Collection*

Computer
Index
Required? — Yes → Make
Computer
Index → Stop

No

Stop

*See Appendix I, A-71--A-112

Library Manual A-52

Subject: Reference Questions.

The Archives Section helps individuals to locate information about the history
of medicine, the history of the Washington University School of Medicine and
the Medical Center, and biographical information about former faculty members
and students:

   1. in those historical materials in the Library Archives.

   2. in monographs and serials in the Library's general collection.

   3. by referring patrons to other sources of information.

For an excellent list of established sources, consult the four pages immediately
following this instruction sheet.

This manual sheet supersedes all previous instruction sheets.

September 1, 1973

CHRONOLOGICAL COVERAGE
OF
PRINCIPAL MEDICAL INDEXES

From - Through	Name of Index	Type of Material Indexed	Arrangement of Material	Separate Alphabetical Index to Classified Indexes
From beginning of printing to date of publication (1679)	Lipenius, Martinus. Bibliotheca Realis Medica,...Frankfurt am Main, Friederic, 1679	Books	Subject	Author
Earliest time to date of publication (1776-88)	Haller, Albrecht von. Bibliotheca Botanica. London, C. Heydinger, 1771-72. 2v. _____. Bibliotheca Chirurgica. Berne, Haller, 1774-75. 2v. _____. Bibliotheca Anatomica. Leyden, Haakiana, 1774-77. 2v. _____. Bibliotheca Medicinae Practicae. Basel, Schweighauser. 1776-88. 4v.	Books, some periodical articles, pamphlets	Subject	Author
Earliest time to date of publication (1808-13)	Ploucquet, Wilhelm G. Literatura Medica Digesta... Tubingae, Apud J.G. Cottam, 1808-09. 4v. Cont. et Suppl. 1. Tubingae, Apud Auctorem. 1813. 226p.	Books, periodicals, dissertations, pamphlets	Subject	
Late eighteenth and early nineteenth century (still living at time of publication) (1830-45)	Callisen, Adolph, C.P. Medicinisches Schrift-steller-Lexicon der Jetzt Lebenden Aerzte, ...Copenhagen [The Author], 1830-45. 33v.	Books, periodicals, dissertations	Author	
Earliest times to 1960's	Index Catalogue	Books, theses, journal articles	Subject, Authors for Books	
1879-Apr. 1899	Index Medicus; Ser. 1	Books, periodicals, theses	Subject	Author and Subject
1900 - 1902	Bibliographia Medica (Index Medicus)	Books, periodicals, theses	Subject	Author
1903 - 1920	Index Medicus Ser. 2	Same	Subject	Author and Subject

From - Through	Name of Index	Type of Material Indexed	Arrangement of Material	Separate Alphabetical Index to Classified Indexes
1914 - 1917	Index Medicus, Ser. 2, Supp. Volume	Limited to Military Medicine	Subject	
1921 - 1926	Index Medicus, Ser. 3	Books, Periodicals, Theses	Subject	Author
1916 - 1926	Quarterly Cumulative Index	Periodicals	Author & Subject	
1927 - 1956	Quarterly Cumulative Index Medicus	Periodicals	Author & Subject	
a. 1941 - 1950 b. 1950 - 1959 (new format)	Current List of Medical Literature	Periodicals	a. By table of contents b. By subject	Author & Subject
1960 +	Index Medicus	Periodicals	Subject & Author	
19 Century	Royal Society. Catalog of Scientific Papers. London, Society, 1863-1899	Periodical Articles	Author	
1955 +	Bibliography of Medical Reviews	Review Articles	Varies	Sometimes published separately; sometimes as part of Index Medicus. Cumulated volume contains v. 1-6, 1955-1961

SOME AMERICAN MEDICAL BIOGRAPHICAL WORKS
(arranged by chronological coverage)

Author	Title	Date of publication	Period Covered	Notes
Thacher, J.	American Medical Biography. 2v.	1828	From colonization to date of publication	Alphabetical with supplement also arranged alphabetically; Contains portraits and sketch of history of medicine
Williams, S.W.	American Medical Biography	1845	Those who died after publication of Thacher	Alphabetical
Kelly, H.A. Burrage, W.L.	Cyclopedia of American Medical Biography. 2v.	1912	Deceased physicians and surgeons 1610-1910	Alphabetical
	American Medical Biographies	1920	Brings preceding to 1919 - some deletions	Alphabetical
	Dictionary of American Medical Biography	1928	Brings preceding to 1927 - some deletions	Alphabetical
Stone, R.F.	Biography of Eminent American Physicians and Surgeons	1894	Last half of 19 century; Supplement to Kelly	Index of portraits, biographies, and geographical coverage; Supplement not alphabetically arranged; Essay on History of Medicine in America; and medical education
Watson, I.A.	Physicians and Surgeons of America	1896	Men then living	No arrangement; Portraits, biographies, locality index; Contains an alphabetical name index
Atkinson, W.B.	Physicians and Surgeons of U.S.	1878	19 Century	Haphazard, but with good name, locality and subject index; Strong in genealogy
	Biographical Dictionary of Contemporary American Physicians and Surgeons	1880	2d edition of preceding	
Walsh, James	History of Medicine in New York	1919	From early times to World War I	v. 4-5, biographies and lists of publications

CURRENT BIOGRAPHICAL INFORMATION ABOUT PHYSICIANS

Author	Title	Period Covered	Notes
	American Medical Directory	1906 +	All legally quali-fied U.S. & Canadian physicians
	Directory of Medical Specialists	1939 +	Diplomates of Amer-ican Specialty Boards
	American Men and Women of Science	1906 +	"Who's Who" type of information. Physical & Biol. Sciences, Social & Behavioral Sciences
Amer. College of Surgeons	Directory	1953 +	Triennial
/General Medical Council/	Medical Register	1859 +	Alphabetic. All legally qualified British physicians
	Medical Directory	1845 +	Geographic & alpha-betic--includes pub-lications-British
	Indian Medical Directory	1945 +	Irregular
	Guide Rosenwald, Medical et Pharmaceutique	1887 -	Annual. Physicians & pharmacists--geo-graphic & alphabetical

NON-CURRENT BIOGRAPHICAL INFORMATION ABOUT PHYSICIANS

Author	Title	Period Covered	Notes
	Polk's Medical Register and Directory of North America	1886-1915	1st-13th eds.
Munk, William	The Roll of the Royal College of Physicians of London	1518-1825	Arranged chronolog-ically, with name and subject index
Brown, G. H.	Lives of the Fellows of the Royal College of Physicians of London	1826-1925	
Plarr, Victor G.	Lives of the Fellows of the Royal College of Surgeons of England	1843-1930	Alphabetic
Power, D'Arcy Le Fanu, William R.	Lives of the Fellows	1930-1951	

Library Manual A-57

Subject: The Historical Reference Collection.

The Historical Reference Collection consists of two parts: (1) a number of books
and book-manuscripts about the history of the Medical Center which are frequently
used for reference purposes, and (2) the Historical Pamphlet File, a collection of
pamphlets and newspaper clippings about the history of medicine and the history of
the Washington University Medical Center.   The pamphlets and newspaper clippings
are in file folders which are arranged alphabetically by subject.   They have been
gathered together in one location to provide easier access to the valuable historical
information they contain.

This manual sheet supersedes all previous instruction sheets.

August 1, 1978

Library Manual A-58

Subject: The Historical Reference File.

The Historical Reference File consists of information collected to answer reference questions. The information is arranged alphabetically in file folders and is divided into two sections: 1) Persons and 2) Subjects. Each person or subject has its own file folder. The detailed information gathered to answer one reference question is thus readily available to answer future reference questions on the same subject.

This manual sheet supersedes all previous instruction sheets.

August 1, 1978

Library Manual A-59

Subject: Library Annex Reference and Circulation Records.

A. Library Annex Reference Requests.

   1. Requests concerning the Archives Collection (exclusive of instructions
       in Library resources) are entered on form Number 72 (a sample of which
       follows this sheet).

   2. Requests for Serials in Archives are entered on form Number 81 (a sample
       of which follows this sheet).

   3. Requests for Rare Books are handled by the Rare Book Librarian.

   4. Requests for those Books and Journals which are part of the Library's
       general collection are handled by the Circulation Assistant.

B. Archives Circulation Register.

    The Archives Circulation Register (see form Number 70 following this sheet) is
    a temporary record of all items removed from the Archives Collection.

C. Library Annex Monthly Report.

    All reference request information (see A above) is entered in statistical form
    on a running tally basis. At the end of each month the statistics are typed
    on the Library Annex Monthly Report form (see Number 74 following this sheet),
    and sent to the Assistant Librarian for her approval and inclusion in the
    Library's Monthly Report. Definitions on the back of Number 74 explain the
    various categories of records held at the Library Annex.

D. Library Annex Annual Report.

    Statistical information for the Library Annex Annual Report is cumulated from
    the preceding twelve months and the results are also entered on form Number 74
    the title of which is then changed to read "Library Annex Annual Report" instead
    of "Library Annex Monthly Report". The narrative portion is likewise attached
    to this form and the results forwarded to the Assistant Librarian.

This manual sheet supersedes all previous instruction sheets.

August 1, 1978

WASHINGTON UNIVERSITY
SCHOOL OF MEDICINE LIBRARY
ARCHIVES

ARCHIVAL REFERENCE REQUEST - ARCHIVAL MATERIAL

Patron Information

Name: Position:

Dept: Address:

Phone:

Archivist: Date:

Staff Use

Instructions in Library Resources: (Indicate only statistical information on the
LIBRARY ANNEX MONTHLY REPORT)

Subject Searches:

Other Services (Including photocopies and microfilm prints)

Patron Use

Record Group #   Title:

Faculty Collection #   Title:

Private Collection #   Title:

Other Sources:

Subject Information

WASHINGTON UNIVERSITY
SCHOOL OF MEDICINE LIBRARY
ARCHIVES

ARCHIVAL REFERENCE REQUEST - SERIALS IN ARCHIVES

NAME: _____   POSITION: _____

DEPT: _____   ADDRESS: _____

PHONE: _____   _____

ARCHIVIST: _____   DATE: _____

SERIALS IN ARCHIVES:

Title: _____

_____

Volume: _____   Pages: _____

Year: _____   Month: _____

Reference Only: _____

Date Charged Out: _____   In: _____

WASHINGTON UNIVERSITY
SCHOOL OF MEDICINE LIBRARY
ARCHIVES

CIRCULATION REGISTER

ITEM #	NAME OF PERSON	DESCRIPTION OF ITEM	DATE REMOVED	DATE RETURNED

WASHINGTON UNIVERSITY SCHOOL OF MEDICINE LIBRARY ANNEX - MONTHLY REPORT

CATEGORIES	MEDICAL CENTER PERSONNEL			NON-MEDICAL CENTER PERSONNEL			TOTAL
	FACULTY	LIBRARY STAFF	STUDENTS	PHONE	MAIL	PERSON	
1. Staff Use							
1. Instructions in Library resources							
2. Subject search							
3. Other services							
2. Patron Use							
1. Record Groups							
2. Faculty Collections							
3. Private Collections							
4. Serials in Archives							
5. Rare Books							
6. Books and Journals							
TOTAL							

MONTH _____

DEFINITIONS OF CATEGORIES LISTED ON LIBRARY ANNEX MONTHLY REPORT

1. <u>Staff use</u> includes the following activities:

   (1) <u>Instruction in Library resources</u> includes the following types of questions: What does the Archives or Rare Book Collection contain? What Books and Journals are shelved at the Library Annex? How do I go about using these materials?

   (2) <u>Subject searches</u> are requests for information about a particular topic-- e.g.: Does the Archives have correspondence between Dr. Green and Dr. Smith concerning pneumonia experiments performed in 1872? Did my grandfather graduate in the class of 1894? Was Dr. Wilson ever a faculty member at a St. Louis Medical College during the nineteenth century?

   (3) <u>Other services</u> include bibliographic verifications and requests that do not fit categories 1 or 2.

2. <u>Patron use</u> includes the following sources:

   (1) <u>Archival Record Groups</u> include the publications, reports, memoranda, correspondence, and other administrative records of the Departments or other divisions of the Washington University School of Medicine, its adjacent Medical Center, or its predecessor institutions.

   (2) <u>Archival Faculty Collections</u> includes the publications, official and personal papers, pictures, memorabilia, and other records of faculty members of the School of Medicine, its adjacent Medical Center, or its predecessor institutions.

   (3) <u>Archival Private Collections</u> include the publications, official and personal papers, pictures, memorabilia, and other records of individual or organizattions <u>not</u> connected with the School of Medicine, its adjacent Medical Center, or its predecessor institutions.

   (4) <u>Serials in Archives</u> are those journals kept in the Archives because they are important in the history of science and medicine, the history of the Medical Center, or connected with the work of the Archivist or Rare Book Librarian.

   (5) <u>Rare Books</u> are the monographs cataloged with the prefixes X, XX, Becker or C.I.D. Permission to charge out these books from the Library must be obtained from the Librarian or the Rare Book Librarian.

   (6) <u>Books and Journals</u>: Books include those monographs classified according to the Dewey Decimal system, the Library Annex reference collection, and certain pre-1965 books received as gifts by the Library. Journals include older journals, little-used titles which have ceased publication or to which the Library no longer subscribes, and the pre-1960 holdings of a few current titles. Books and Journals are shelved in the stacks at the Medical Library Annex.

3. Other services, including bibliographic verifications and unusual questions, should be listed here:

   _____

   _____

   _____

FLOW CHART 19

USE OF ARCHIVES COLLECTION

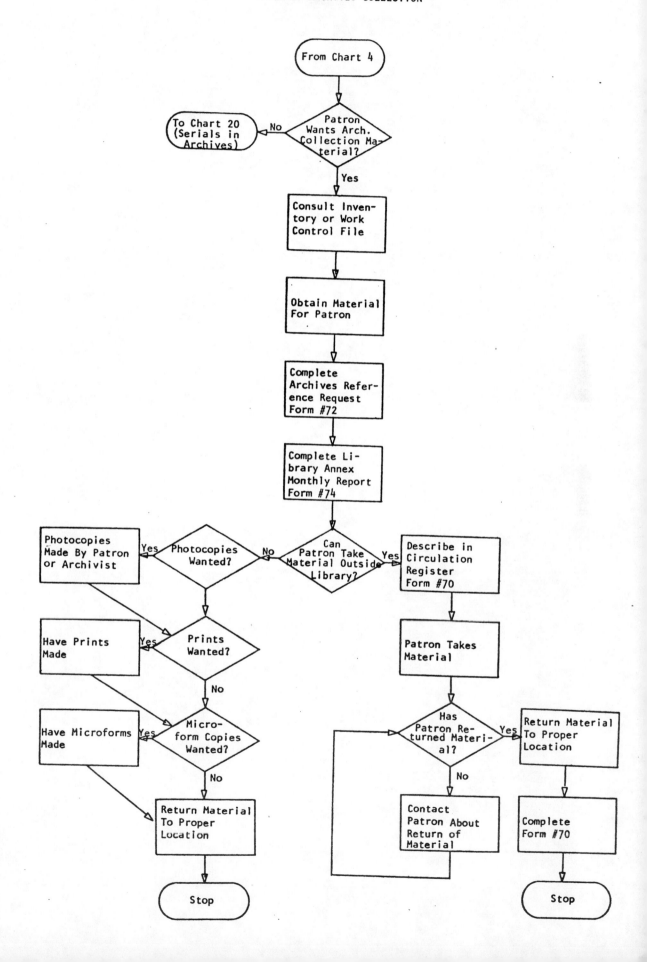

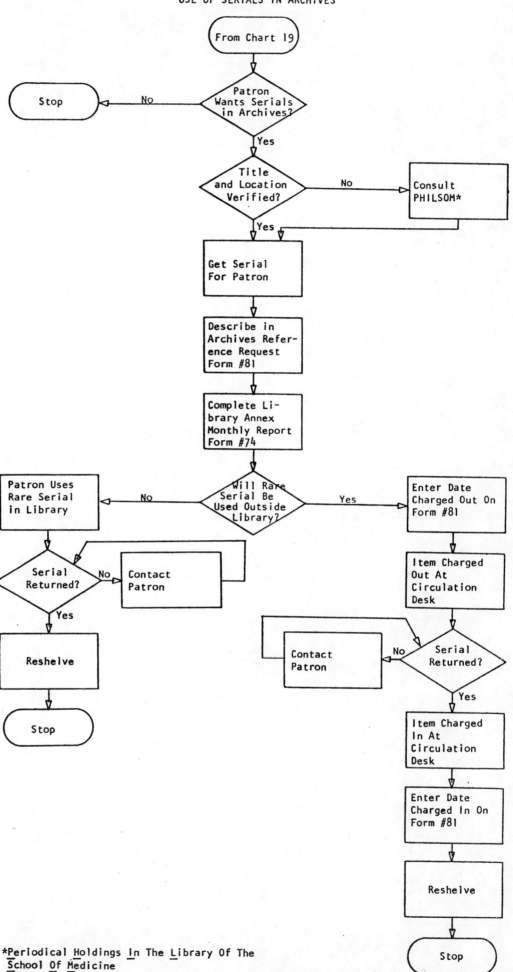

Library Manual A-67

Subject: Exhibits.

The Archivist, in cooperation with other members of the Library Staff helps in
the preparation and display of Library exhibits. The Archivist keeps written
documentation of all exhibits for future reference purposes.

This manual sheet supersedes all previous instruction sheets.

September 1, 1973

Library Manual A-68

Subject: Oral History Program.

A. Objectives.

One of the continuing problems in archival administration is the need to collect historical information while it is still available; especially information that exists only in the memories of older members of the parent institution of which the archives is a part. With this need in mind, the Library started an oral history program in the fall of 1969. Its objectives are:

1. To document the history of Washington University School of Medicine and the Washington University Medical Center.

2. To document the outstanding scientific achievements of Washington University School of Medicine faculty members in their particular medical specialties.

3. To make the contents of the oral history interviews accessible to researchers through the Oral History Computer Index.

B. Procedures.

1. In consultation with the Librarian, the Archivist will systematically determine which persons should be interviewed and what topics should be discussed.

2. To be satisfactorily prepared for an interview the Archivist will gather appropriate biographical data and curriculum vitae about a prospective interviewee.

3. The Archivist will contact the prospective interviewee about recording his reminiscences on sound tape. Prospective topics are then discussed, and interview arrangements are made.

4. For best results an interview should be limited to 60 minutes. Additional interviews can be held if necessary.

5. The interview should normally be held in the Archivist's office, but may be held with the interviewee at any mutually convenient place.

6. The Statement of Gift for Oral History Interviews, Form Number 82, must be signed by the Donor and the Librarian. The Donor may impose such additional restrictions on the use of the magnetic tape recordings and/or transcripts of the interview(s) as he wishes and Form Number 82 will be modified according to the Donor's wishes.

7. The tape recorder and accessory equipment used in these interviews are normally stored in the Archives Office. Operating instructions are attached to the recorder.

(continued on next page)

Library Manual A-69

Subject: Oral History Program (continued).

8. Upon completion of an interview the tape reel should be indexed through the
    Oral History Computer Index. For further details see Library Manual Ap-
    pendix III, A-118--A-134.

9. For further information on oral history programs and techniques, consult the
    American Association for State and Local History's Technical Leaflet 35,
    "Tape-Recording Local History" by William G. Tyrrell, and Willa K. Baum,
    Oral History for the Local Historical Society. (Nashville, American Asso-
    ciation for State and Local History, 1971).

This manual sheet supersedes all previous instruction sheets.

August 1, 1978

WASHINGTON UNIVERSITY

SCHOOL OF MEDICINE
ST. LOUIS, MISSOURI 63110

THE LIBRARY
4580 SCOTT AVENUE
(314) 367-6400 EXT. 3711
TWX 1-910-761-2165

STATEMENT OF GIFT

ORAL HISTORY INTERVIEWS

I, _____give to the Washington University School

of Medicine Library Archives the magnetic tape recordings of the interview(s) held

on _____between _____

and myself, together with any transcript(s) that may be made from these recordings,

("the material") subject to the following conditions:

1) The material shall be available to scientists, historians and other
   qualified scholars who wish to use them for research purposes.

2) Although any portion of the material may be copied, it may be pub-
   lished only with the express written permission of the Librarian,
   Washington University School of Medicine Library, 4580 Scott Avenue,
   St. Louis, Missouri, 63110.

_____
Donor

Accepted:

_____
Date

_____
Librarian - Washington University
School of Medicine Library

_____
Date

Subject: Preparing an Acquired Collection for Microfilming.

If not already done:

A. All staples, pins, clips, tape, or other adhesives must be removed from the documents before they can be filmed. After microfilming they may be restapled with monel rustproof staples.

B. All folders must be arranged in some logical order.

C. The total number of microfilm images must be counted or estimated. To estimate this figure, a rough rule of thumb is:

    1. There are 1150 images per document box (Hollinger box).

    2. There are 4740 images per cabinet file drawer or large transfer case, (both normally contain 2 cubic feet of records).

This manual sheet supersedes all previous instruction sheets.

August 1, 1978

Library Manual Appendix I, A-72

Subject: Indexing an Acquired Collection for Microfilming.

Based on experience acquired in microfilming the Evarts A. Graham and Joseph
Erlanger Collections, it has been determined that <u>each document box should be
filmed on a separate reel because this practice permits</u>:

A.   <u>An accurate image estimate for the entire collection</u> as each reel will contain
     an approximate average of 1140 images (assuming the bulk of the collection is
     8 1/2" x 11" papers).

B.   <u>The Archivist to thoroughly plan the indexing of each reel</u> by using a standard
     form known as a Microfilm Operation and Inspection Control Record (M-14) sold
     by the Remington Rand Corporation.

C.   <u>Precise and lucid instructions to the camera operator</u> including:

     1.   The Reel Completion Record M-15. The M-15 is also sold by Remington
          Rand Corporation.

     2.   Handwritten instructions to the operator.

This manual sheet supersedes all previous instruction sheets.

September 1, 1973

Library Manual Appendix I, A-73

Subject: Targeting an Acquired Collection for Microfilming.

A. The use of standardized microfilm targets

    1. Provides uniformity, clarity, and neatness among microfilm targets.

    2. Prevents needless duplication of similar targets.

B. Standardized targets may be divided into the following types:

    1. Non-repetitive targets (A-74) which can be used for one collection only.

    2. Repetitive targets (A-75--A-106) which can be used for any collection.

    3. Handwritten targets (A-107 is a sample) which are unique targets for individual documents or folders, and are made with magic marker pencils, white paper, and a special cardboard cutout (A-108).

This manual sheet supersedes all previous instruction sheets.

September 1, 1973

MARGARET G. SMITH

COLLECTION

1896-1970

DATE FILMED

NO COPIES
TO BE MADE
WITHOUT
WRITTEN
PERMISSION

FACULTY

COLLECTION

RECORD

GROUP

RECORD SERIES

RECORD SUBSERIES

PRIVATE

COLLECTION

SUBGROUP 1
PUBLICATIONS

SUBGROUP 2
BOUND PAPERS

SUBGROUP 3
LOOSE PAPERS

SUBGROUP 4
CARD FILES

SUBGROUP 5

PICTORIAL RECORDS

SUBGROUP 6
MEMORABILIA

SUBGROUP 7
SOUND RECORDINGS

SUBGROUP 8

CARTOGRAPHIC

RECORDS

AND

BLUEPRINTS

SUBGROUP 9

MICROFORM

RECORDS

TITLE PAGE ONLY

FILMED

TITLE PAGE

AND

PAGES

FILMED

REEL NUMBER

REEL NUMBER

END

REEL NUMBER

INDEX

INDEX
TO
THIS
REEL

END
OF
INDEX

END

OF

INDEX

APPENDIX

THE FOLLOWING IMAGES HAVE BEEN REFILMED BECAUSE THEY WERE
UNREADABLE UPON INSPECTION OF THE ORIGINAL MICROFILM REEL.

END
OF
APPENDIX

CORRECTION

THE FOLLOWING

DOCUMENTS

HAVE BEEN

REFILMED FOR

GREATER

ACCURACY

ILLEGIBLE

DIFFICULT

TO

READ

CONTINUED

FILMED

IN

SECTIONS

DO NOT

FILM

THESE

DOCUMENTS

XIII INTERNATIONAL
PHYSIOLOGICAL CONGRESS
BOSTON. [AUG. 19-23, 1929
FOR RELATED PHOTO-
GRAPH OF CONGRESS
SEE PICTURE #27]

Library Manual Appendix I, A-108

Subject: Outline of Cardboard Cut-Out Used to Make Handwritten Microfilm Targets.

Library Manual Appendix I, A-109

Subject: Library Microfilm Work Chart.

When the Library decides to film a collection the attached Work Chart (see form
Number 73 following this instruction sheet) must be used to keep track of the work
done.

This manual sheet supersedes all previous instruction sheets.

August 1, 1978

MICROFILM WORK CHART

for Camera Operators

Year

Date	Col-lection Name	Reel #	Begin Count	End Count	Operator	Image Count	Minutes Worked	Description of Material

Library Manual Appendix I, A-111

Subject: Microfilm Processing, Inspection, and Appendix Retakes.

A. Processing.

    When the documents in a new collection have been microfilmed, the completed
    master negative reels must be processed by a commercial microfilm dealer.
    The processing costs are usually included in the initial purchase cost of the
    film.

B. Inspection.

    Detailed reel inspection by the Archivist is essential for good microfilm
    results. Each reel must be inspected for fogged documents, improper light
    density, missing documents, improper targeting, etc. Errors should be
    noted on the M-14 Form for each reel.

C. Appendix Retakes.

    Once errors are noted and recorded, the original documents should be re-
    filmed where necessary, inspected, and spliced as an appendix at the begin-
    ning of each reel. This procedure alerts all patrons to necessary corrections
    when they are viewing the main portion of the reel.

This manual sheet supersedes all previous instruction sheets.

September 1, 1973

Library Manual Appendix I, A-112

Subject: Microfilm Prints.

Once a new collection has been microfilmed, a print of all film should be made for use by Library patrons and the original master negative stored in a fire-proof vault as a security copy.

  1. The original copy is thus protected against destruction or loss.

  2. New prints can be readily made by a commercial dealer from the original master negative.

This manual sheet supersedes all previous instruction sheets.

November 1, 1973

WASHINGTON UNIVERSITY
SCHOOL OF MEDICINE LIBRARY

Archivist

JOB DESCRIPTION
August 1978

Introduction and Background

The Library of Washington University School of Medicine serves as the information resource for the entire Washington University Medical Center in St. Louis,
and by courtesy extends consulting privileges to non-affiliated biomedical professionals. Through the Regional Medical Library, and through local cooperative
ventures such as the Higher Education Coordinating Council, it accepts regional
and national responsibilities. It makes its computer expertise available to
others by running a network of serials control for a number of medical libraries
through the nation, and it sells many of its computer-produced products.

The Library is divided into the following sections: Office of the Librarian,
Technical Services, Public Services, PHILSOM and Machine Projects. The Archives
Section is part of the Office of the Librarian.

The Archives Section is responsible for acquiring, preserving, listing and
making useful the records of scientists and of the School. It publicizes its
collections through talks, articles, exhibits and other means. It conducts an
Oral History project to supplement the written records and the artifacts in the
collection and indexes the oral history interviews by computer to make the contents accessible to researchers. Its basic finding guides are kept in its confines and are not placed in the public catalog. It publishes a computer index
to its Beaumont Collection.

Reporting and Guidelines

The Archivist reports directly to the Librarian. Guidelines include the
Library's Manual of Operation, the Archives Procedural Manual, works on the
history of science and medicine and on general history, and texts on archival
management.

Duties

1. Collects additional important manuscript and archival collections.

2. Organizes new archival collections according to the principle of provenance
   and the principle of original order. Prepares inventories to these
   collections.

3. Provides for the preservation of manuscript collections by:

   a. supervising the microfilm camera operator in her work.

(continued on next page)

  b. inspecting the microfilm master negatives to ensure the microfilm is of high quality.

  c. supervising the placement of material in acid-free containers properly labeled and shelved.

4. Aids readers in their use of the archival collections.

5. Answers some historical reference questions; others are handled by Rare Book Librarian, or Librarian.

6. Conducts the Oral History Program of the Library; abstracts and indexes the oral history interviews for the Oral History Computer Index.

7. Publicizes the availability of the manuscript collections for use.

8. Explains archival resources and procedures to visitors and other interested persons.

9. Supervises the work of the Archives Library Assistant.

10. In conjunction with other members of the staff, prepares or helps with the preparation of Library exhibits, <u>Library Notes</u>, <u>Library Guide</u>, and other publications.

11. Insures that the Library Archives is receiving all important publications of the Medical Center that relate to its history.

12. Reports on archival practices and operations.

13. Developes increasing skill in the handling of archival materials through experience, education, and reading.

14. Participates in medical and archival professional organizations.

15. Performs other duties as assigned.

<u>Effects of Work</u>

The collection and preservation of the primary records of science are essential for checking facts, for determining the methods of science, and for studying the history of ideas. Unlike political and economic life which has evolved formal documents of record, scientific endeavor has rarely preserved the bases of its work. For this reason the knowledge of how scientists came to their conclusions, what hypotheses they tested and rejected, who influenced them and whom they influenced, and what institutions they molded is very meager. Because science exalts anonymity, it is necessary to make an effort to obtain its personalia, but without them only part of the story of scientific development is known. And once the material has been obtained, it must be arranged usefully for scholars, indexed, and preserved for future generations. Scientific papers are unique items which, when lost, are irrevocably gone from mankind's store of knowledge.

(continued on next page)

Requirements of Incumbent

The incumbent must have a college degree, preferably in history or science, and either additional courses in these subjects, in archival administration, in the history of science, or in librarianship. He must be interested in serving people, have the ability to get along with others, be able to write and speak clearly and effectively. He must be able to organize and carry out plans.

WASHINGTON UNIVERSITY
SCHOOL OF MEDICINE LIBRARY

Archives Library Assistant II

Job Description
August 1978

Introduction and Background

The Library of Washington University School of Medicine serves as the information resource for the entire Washington University Medical Center in St. Louis, and by courtesy extends consulting privileges to non-affiliated biomedical professionals. Through the Regional Medical Library, and through local cooperative ventures such as the Higher Education Coordinating Council, it accepts regional and national responsibilities. It makes its computer expertise available to others by running a network of serials control for a number of medical libraries throughout the nation, and it sells many of its computer-produced products.

The Library is divided into the following sections: Office of the Librarian, Technical Services, Public Services, PHILSOM and Machine Methods Project. The Archives Section is part of the Office of the Librarian.

The Archives Section is responsible for acquiring, preserving, listing and making useful the records of scientists and of the School. It publicizes its collections through talks, articles, exhibits, and other means. It conducts an Oral History project to supplement the written records and the artifacts in the collection and indexes the oral history interviews by computer to make the contents accessible to patrons. Its basic finding guides are kept in its confines and are not placed in the public catalog. It publishes a computer index to its Beaumont Collection.

Reporting and Guidelines

The Archives Library Assistant reports directly to the Archivist, who examines her work in detail. There is a Washington University Archives Manual for a good part of the work; in addition the past indexes and calendars of the Archives Section serve as examples of format and style.

1. Types necessary reports, letters and inventories from handwritten copy.

2. Assists the Archivist in organizing manuscript collections.

3. Helps to prepare manuscript collections and special projects for microfilming by making microfilm targets.

4. Operates the microfilm camera when archival collections are filmed.

5. Types abstracting and indexing forms for key punchers for use in oral history index; transcribes oral history interviews from tapes, when necessary.

6. Assists the Rare Book Librarian in his work.

7. Answers telephone and helps caller, when possible, or directs call to the Archivist, Rare Book Librarian, or Circulation Page.

(continued on next page)

8. Fills orders, makes invoices, and keeps all necessary records for the sale of <u>Archival Procedural Manuals</u>.

9. Assumes responsibility for the administration of the Library Annex when the Archivist and the Rare Book Librarian are not in the building.

10. Indexes pictures for the Archives Picture Index.

11. Assists Library Annex patrons in the use of the journals and books in the stacks, checking out and in circulated books and journals when the circulation page is not present.

12. Performs other duties as assigned.

Effects of Work

Archival collections are usually large numbers of individual written or printed matter, which must be described in blocks in finding aids and then indexed directly onto the file folder or box in which the documents are housed. Much of this work is of purely a clerical nature, yet without it, it would be difficult if not impossible to locate all the material in the Archives pertaining to a question. To do the work accurately, neatly, and quickly makes it possible for scholars to use the collections with ease and dispatch.

The preservation of archival material is vital to our knowledge of the way in which science developed; mostly, archival materials are unique items which, when lost, are irrevocably gone from mankind's store of knowledge. The proper microfilming, housing and handling of the documents is therefore extremely important.

Requirements of Incumbent

Must be a high school graduate with knowledge of typing (at least 40 words per minute), accurate, neat, able to write well, careful with manuscripts and objects, and able to learn to use a microfilm camera so that only a small percent of re-takes are necessary. Must not object to working alone for long periods of times.

Subject: Oral History Computer Index.

The Oral History Computer Index is a computerized index to oral history tape recordings. The index indicates where on a timed tape any subject is discussed. This allows the user to turn directly to that portion of the tape, rather than have to listen to the entire interview until the desired section is reached.

The Oral History Computer Index consists of two sections: the first section contains the abstracts for all interviews and indicates the location, interview number, date and duration of the interview; the second section contains the index terms for all interviews and lists the subject phrase, location, interview number, reel, side, duration and interview name. Examples of both sections are given in Appendix III, A-119 and A-120.

The indexing scheme utilizes main headings which are subject phrases arranged alphabetically. Subheading phrases are arranged under mainheadings by their chronology within the voice tape. Each subheading points to a short abstract of the contents of the oral history interview and the exact spot on the tape where the particular subheading is discussed.

This manual sheet supersedes all previous instruction sheets.

August 1, 1978

ORAL HISTORY INDEX

PAGE 1

LOC: 1 INTERVIEW-NO: 22 DATE: 051376 DURATION: 45:20
HERBERT ANDERSON TALKS ABOUT PROFESSORS GRAHAM, EVARTS, JEAN V. COO... AND HIS EARLY CHILDHOOD. HE DISCUSSES CHANGES IN MEDICAL EDUCATION IN CALIFORNIA. BARNEY BROOKS AND... HIS INTERNSHIP AND NAVY. HE SUBSEQUENT WORKING LIFE AND SURGEON. HE HAS STARTED HIS PRACTICE IN ABDOMINAL SURGERY. AT STUDIES ABROAD FOR 12 YEARS. HE THE UNIVERSITY AND THE EVEN IN THE METHODS USED AT THE UNIVERSITY VIENNA.

LOC: 1 INTERVIEW-NO: 23 DATE: 051376 DURATION: 58:00
ADAM BOYD, JR. TALKS ABOUT HIS FAMILY AND CHILDHOOD, AND HE OFFICER HIS TRAINING PROGRAM AT THE MEDICAL SCHOOL. BOYD DROPPED OUT OF MEDICAL UNIVERSITY. RETURNING, HIS DEGREE WAS WASHINGTON. MEDICINE. WHEN HIS RETURN THE COMPLETE. WORKED FOR... SENIOR YEAR IN ORIENTATION WITH THEIR PRODUCTS. GOING HIS EXPERIENCE. BARNEY BOYD. BROOKS. EVARTS. GRAHAM. INSTRUCTORS. SACHS. INFLUENCE OF BARNEY BROOKS. DUE UP PRIVATE PRACTICE IN HOUSTON AND THEIR SPECIALIZED IN MEDICINE. TALKS OF YEARS AND THEIR EFFECT ON HIS PRACTICE.

LOC: 1 INTERVIEW-NO: 31 DATE: 051277 DURATION: 41:30
BRENT L. PARKER... DISCUSSES MEDICAL EDUCATION. EARLY IN THE MID-1970'S. MEDICARE. CONTRAST. EUTHANASIA. AS A PROBLEMS OF THE 1950'S. 1970'S. MALPRACTICE. CARTER. YEARLY PARK. RECOMMENDATIONS ON THAT THE HOSPITAL. SEXUAL PRACTICES. OF THE PRIVATE MEDICAL COMPETITION. SCHOOLS. LATE AUDITS OF THE INFLUENCE OF BARRY WOOD AND JOHN SMITH PARKER'S CAREER.

LOC: 1 INTERVIEW-NO: 32 DATE: 051377 DURATION: 63:10
JOHN... DAVIDSON... DISCUSSES MEDICAL EDUCATION IN THE MID-1970'S. SINCE AS PROBLEMS OF THE HOSPITAL. 1950'S, AND MALPRACTICE. CARTER. DAVIDSON TALKS ABOUT HIS FELLOWSHIP AT PRESIDENT CARTER'S RECOMMENDATIONS THAT NOT EXCEED 9% YEARLY. DAVIDSON RECEIVED MALLINCKRODT FOUNDATION OF THAT RESULTED TO DECREASE THE AMOUNT OF GRANT DAMAGE. HEART ATTACK. DECREASE THE SIZE OF MYOCARDIAL INFARCTION RECEIVED HYPERBARIC OXYGEN WHILE DIRECTOR OF DIVISION OF HYPERBARIC MEDICINE DONE AT ST. LUKE'S HOSPITAL IN ST. LOUIS.

LOC: 1 INTERVIEW-NO: 14 DATE: 041574 DURATION: 39:00
JOHN... PIERCE, M.C. TALKS ABOUT THE LIFE AND WORK OF ALFRED GOLDMAN. CHICKBECKWITH. MEDICAL WORK UNDER JOSEPH ERLANGER. TALKS ABOUT HIS UNDER THREE IN CALIFORNIA PHYSIOLOGY. ALL PHYSICIAN. ANZGELVENS, TALKS OF GOLDMAN. HYPERVENTILATION. WORKED CLASS AND WAS THE TEACHERS OF... HYPERTRIBUTION. ALSO TALKS THREE YEARS IN... GOLDMAN AND HIS... TRIAL DISEASE AND LUNG DISEASE AS... IS ALFRED GOLDMAN BOOK AWARD WAS OCCUPATION BY HIS... THE OUTSTANDING GRADUATING SENIOR IN PULMONARY DISEASE.

LOC: 1 INTERVIEW-NO: 16 DATE: 051675 DURATION: 103:05
BECKWITH... HOWORTH, TERRY... DISCUSSES HIS WORK AND THE ORTHOPEDIC ANATOMY... INTRODUCED PRACTICAL ORTHOPEDIC ANATOMY WHILE ANATOMY. HOWORTH'S WRITING EXPERIENCES. HOSPITAL. JOURNAL HOWORTH'S ARTICLES AND TEXTBOOKS. MEDICAL PERIODICAL. HOWORTH. PICTURED FOR... ORTHOPEDIC SOCIETY. IN AMERICAN AND ORTHOPEDIC INTERNATIONAL. AND HIS MEDICAL ASSOCIATIONS. RECREATIONAL ACTIVITIES. MEDICAL INTERESTS. HOWORTH

LOC: 1 INTERVIEW-NO: 17 DATE: 051675 DURATION: 47:45
JEROME... LEVY. TALKS ABOUT... DISCUSSES HIS MEDICAL CAREER IN FIELD OF GASTROENTEROLOGY. THE JEFFERSON LECTURESHIP IN GASTROENTEROLOGY. AT UNIVERSITY OF ARKANSAS SCHOOL. DISCUSSES ARTICLES HE HAS WRITTEN, HIS MEMBERS OF THE CLASS OF 1925, AND FELLOW

LOC: 1 INTERVIEW-NO: 18 DATE: 051675 DURATION: 23:20
L. E... HIEBERT DISCUSSES FAMILY AND CHILDHOOD INFLUENCES ON HIS FACULTY. B.K. BLAIR. TALKS OF... ACHS. GRAHAM OF EVARTS. AND THE INFLUENTIAL HIEBERT TALKS OF HIS TRAINING AND EXPERIENCE IN FIELD OF PLASTIC SURGERY, AND HIS WORK WITH REHABILITATION OF BEARING PORTIONS OF THE BODY. REMOVAL OF SCARS FROM...

ORAL HISTORY INDEX

SUBJECT PHRASE	LOC	INT. NO.	REEL	SIDE	DURATION	INTERVIEW NAME
ABBOTT, LERCY C.						
PETERSON, WALTER R., INFLUENCED BY	1	25	3	2	161:20-161:35	WALTER R. PETERSON
ACCEPTANCE BY THE HOSPITALS; DIFFICULTIES OF	1	33	8	1	117:20-118:40	FRANCES STEWART
ACUPUNCTURE						
GREER, EDWIN D., COMMENTS ON	1	24	3	2	123:20-127:00	EDWIN D. GREER
ADMISSIONS COMMITTEE, W.U.S.M.						
CRITERIA FOR SELECTING STUDENTS	1	21	3	2	25:30-31:50	WILLIAM B. PARKER
ALKALINE PH IN URINE DUE TO HYPERVENTILATION	1	14	3	1	43:20-43:30	JOHN A. PIERCE
ALKALOSIS, CARBON DIOXIDE PRODUCTION IN LUNGS LEADING TO MARKED	1	14	3	1	46:35-46:40	JOHN A. PIERCE
ALLBROOK, DAVID						
DEPARTMENT HEAD OF ANATOMY, MAKERERER UNIVERSITY COLLEGE	1	9	2	1	18:00-18:30	MILDRED TROTTER
DEPARTMENT HEAD OF ANATOMY, MAKERERE UNIVERSITY COLLEGE	1	9	2	1	19:00-19:45	MILDRED TROTTER
DEPARTMENT HEAD OF ANATOMY, MAKERERER UNIVERSITY COLLEGE	1	9	2	1	21:00-21:45	MILDRED TROTTER
ALLEN, EC						
TROTTER, MILDRED, TALKS ABOUT	1	10	2	1	53:30-53:40	MILDRED TROTTER
TROTTER, MILDRED, TALKS ABOUT	1	10	2	1	55:40-56:50	MILDRED TROTTER
ANATOMICAL STRUCTURES MADE FROM SECTIONS OF POISONOUS GAS VICTIMS AT BASE HOSPITAL 21	1	1	1	1	7:30-7:45	JOSEPH MAGIDSON
ANDERSON, HERBERT A.						
FAMILY AND EARLY CHILDHOOD	1	22	5	2	27:35-30:10	HERBERT ANDERSON
DECISION TO ENTER MEDICINE	1	22	5	2	30:15-32:35	HERBERT ANDERSON
WASHINGTON UNIVERSITY SCHOOL OF MEDICINE	1	22	5	2	33:00-34:20	HERBERT ANDERSON
GRAHAM, EVARTS A., INFLUENCE ON	1	22	5	2	34:40-36:20	HERBERT ANDERSON
SACHS, ERNEST, INFLUENCE ON	1	22	5	2	36:25-38:00	HERBERT ANDERSON
BROOKS, BARNEY, INFLUENCE ON	1	22	5	2	38:10-38:55	HERBERT ANDERSON
COOKE, JEAN V., INFLUENCE ON	1	22	5	2	39:00-39:20	HERBERT ANDERSON

Subject: Oral History Work Control File.

The Oral History Work Control File contains a copy of the oral history
index manual, a list of all of the oral history interviews conducted, a
file folder for each interview, a list of possible future oral history
interviews and blank abstracting and indexing forms.

All information for one interview is kept together in a file folder in the
work control file. Each folder is labeled with the name of the person interviewed and the number of the interview. The information in the file folder
includes the signed oral history statement of gift, a list of questions
asked during the interview, background information, and the completed abstract and indexing forms.

This manual sheet supersedes all previous instruction sheets.

August 1, 1978

Library Manual Appendix III, A-122

Subject: Duplication of Oral History Interviews.

It is necessary to make a reel-to-reel copy of the reel-to-reel tape recorded interview for patron use, security, and indexing purposes.

1. Record the interview on track 1 (See A-123).

2. Record the time sequence on track 2 (See A-125).

3. Read the instructions for duplicating oral history interviews, (A-123). This will explain the jack hook-up between machines.

4. Make a sample recording to check the connections. After about one minute, stop the machines and rewind. Listen to the duplicate and check to see if the sound was recorded correctly. If it was not, recheck the connections and test again. When the sound is correct, rewind both machines, start the duplicating recorder, wait 30 seconds, then start the original tape. The 30 second delay will assure that none of the original is lost on the duplicate in case of tape breakage on the lead strip.

5. Interviews are originally recorded at 1-7/8 ips. It is possible to play the original tape at 7-1/2 ips to lessen duplicating time. Both machines must be at the same speed. When the tapes are finished, the speed can be turned back to 1-7/8 ips and the sound will be normal. It is not necessary to listen to the tapes continuously during duplication. The speaker switch may be turned on only at intervals to make sure the recorder is working properly.

6. Label tapes and tape boxes as soon as recording is finished:

    a. patron copy
    b. reel #
    c. side #
    d. interview # and name of interview

7. Duplicate copies are kept in the archivist's office. Originals are kept in the vault.

This manual sheet supersedes all previous instruction sheets.

August 1, 1978

Subject: How to Duplicate Oral History Interviews.

Reel-to-Reel Duplication

1. Put original tape on tape recorder 1 -- plug in monitor or external speaker output.
2. Turn to channel one when duplicating oral histories.
3. Turn to channel two when duplicating time sequence.
4. Put blank tape on tape recorder 2.
5. Plug in channel one auxiliary input when recording oral histories.
6. When ready to record push in channel one record button and turn to play.
7. Plug in channel two auxiliary input when duplicating time sequence.
8. When ready to record push in channel two record button and turn to play.
9. Turn tape recorder 1 to play.

Reel-to-Cassette Duplication

1. Plug in channel one line output on the reel-to-reel tape recorder containing the original tape.
2. Plug in line or microphone input on the cassette recorder containing the blank tape.
3. Push record and play buttons on the cassette tape recorder.
4. Turn to play on the reel-to-reel tape recorder.

Cassette-to-Reel Duplication

1. Plug into monitor or ear output on the cassette tape recorder containing the original tape.
2. Plug into channel one auxiliary input on the reel-to-reel tape recorder containing the blank tape.
3. Push in channel one record button and turn to play on the reel-to- reel tape recorder.
4. Push play button on the cassette tape recorder.

It may be necessary to monitor the loudness of the voices in some cases and adjust the volume accordingly.

Reel-to-Cassette-to-Cassette Duplication

When it is necessary to make two or more cassette copies from a reel-to-reel tape recording it can be done in the following manner:

1. Hook up the reel-to-reel tape recorder to the cassette tape recorder 1 in the normal way for duplicating reel-to-cassette.
2. Then hook up cassette tape recorder 1 to cassette tape recorder 2 as follows:
    (1) Cassette 1, plug into monitor.
    (2) Cassette 2, plug into microphone.

(continued on next page)

Library Manual Appendix III, A-124

Subject: How to Duplicate Oral History Interviews (continued).

   3. Cassette 2, push record and play buttons.
   4. Cassette 1, push record and play buttons.
   5. Turn to play on the reel-to-reel tape recorder.

This manual sheet supersedes all previous instruction sheets.

August 1, 1978

Library Manual Appendix III, A-125

Subject: Duplicating Time Sequence on to Duplicate Copy of Tapes.

1. Make a master "time-tape" recording listing the minutes and seconds (at
    5 second intervals) on channel two of a reel-to-reel tape recorder.
    This is done by reciting minutes and seconds into the recorder at 5
    second intervals as follows: 5 seconds, 10 seconds, 15 seconds, ...
    55 seconds; one minute, 5 seconds, ten seconds, ... 2 minutes, etc.

2. Set up a jack between two reel-to-reel tape recorders as described in
    duplicating oral history interviews (see A-123). Use channel two on
    both machines. This will allow time and interview to be heard at the
    same time when the duplication is completed.

3. Put original time sequence on tape recorder 1 and turn to track two.

4. Put duplicate copy of interview on tape recorder 2 and turn to track two.

5. Duplication at this point is the same as points 4 and 5 on page A-122.

6. It is very important to remember to check the connections by making a
    sample recording before recording the entire tape.

This manual sheet supersedes all previous instruction sheets.

August 1, 1978

Subject: Indexing Oral History Interviews for the Oral History Computer Index.

1. Search the oral history work control file for background information about the person interviewed and the topics covered by the interview.

2. Make a cover slip (3"x5") which lists the name, number, date and beginning and ending time of the interview.

3. Use 3"x5" slips of paper to record notes.

4. Listen to the interview, listing subjects that will become index terms on the 3"x5" slips. At this point, it is not necessary to listen to the second track and time.

5. After listening to the entire interview and recording index terms, check the proposed terms against those in the most recent Oral History Computer Index (See also A-127). Standardize the index terms whenever possible. Keep the slips in the order they were written (time order).

6. When the index terms are standardized, listen to the tape a second time, using the time track. Note on each slip the beginning and ending time of the index term. This time is used as an address for that particular term.

7. Use the index terms, the background information from the Oral History Work Control File, and information gained by listening to the tape to write an abstract of the interview. The abstract is written in free flow paragraph form.

8. See Instructions for Filling out Abstract and Index Terms Forms (A-128). Transfer the abstract to the Abstracting Form for Oral History Computer Index (A-129). Transfer the index terms to the Indexing Form for Oral History Computer Index (A-131).

9. Use the main heading * for all names and any other terms that will have multiple entries now or which are likely to occur in succeeding interviews. The * tells the computer that all terms with an * must be kept together. When designating a main heading, on the index form, a * in column 9 is necessary.

10. It is important not to have the same time for separate ideas or terms under a main heading. If separate ideas or terms are given the same time under a main heading they will be listed together in one entry.

11. Number each index form in sequence and staple all pages together.

12. Send the forms to keypunching.

13. When the cards and forms are returned from keypunching, mark the interview number on the side of the card deck in pencil.

14. Place the abstract and index forms that have been returned in the file folder for that interview.

15. Place the new cards with all other cards from previous interviews and take them to the Biomedical Computer Lab and run the program.

This manual sheet supersedes all previous instruction sheets.

August 1, 1978

Library Manual Appendix III, A-127

Subject: Examples of Standard Indexing Terms.

This is a partial list of standard indexing terms. For a complete listing,
check the most recent Oral History Computer Index.

1. * Euthanasia vs. Lifesaving equipment (and reverse)

2. * Malpractice mid-1970's
        Doe, John S., comments

3. * Medical education
        Doe, John S., contrast late 1940's (any year) with mid-1970's (any year)

4. * Medical education
        Doe, John S., comments on the mid-1970's (any year)

5. * Medicare in mid-1970's
        Doe, John S.

6. * Doe, John S.   Invert names when they are a main heading
        Smith, Robert, influenced by   or when they are the first words of sub-
                                             heading. Include middle initial when
7. * Smith, Robert   known. Check to see if and how the name
        Doe, John S., influence on   has been used previously.

8. * Philosophy as a physician
        Doe, John S.

"See" and "see also" terms.

9.   Birth control clinics
        See also planned parenthood

10.   Contraceptive clinics   Times for "see" and "see also" must be
        See birth control clinic   0:00-0:00.

11.   Planned parenthood
        See also birth control clinics

12.   High blood pressure
        See hypertension

* means main heading.

This manual sheet supersedes all previous instruction sheets.

August 1, 1978

Library Manual Appendix III, A-128

Subject: Instructions for Filling Out Abstract and Index Term Forms for
          the Oral History Computer Index.

Interview Abstract Form (See A-129 and A-130)

	Spaces
Int. #	1-4
Loc. 010	6-8
Date of interview 061777	13-18
Length of interview # of minutes long 54:25	20-25
Seq. # 01, 02, 03, ...	10-11
Abstract - first line starts at	13-77
second line and subsequent lines start at	16-77

Index Term Form (See A-131 and A-132)

	Spaces
Int. #	1-4
Loc. remains the same for all 011b00	6-11
Name or title of interview	13-43
Int. #	1-4
Loc. 011 (Location 1)	6-8
Side and reel 10008 (side 1 reel 8)	12-16
MH main heading (* on first line only)	9
Seq. # 01, 02, 03, ... keeps all lines of one term	
together	10-11
Position: we use time	17-29
Index terms: first line starts at 30	
second and following lines at 33	
can only go up to 77 (30-77 & 33-77)	

For "see" or "see also" terms, use time of 0:00-0:00

This manual sheet supersedes all previous instruction sheets.

August 1, 1978

ABSTRACTING FORM FOR ORAL HISTORY COMPUTER INDEX

INT. #   DATE   LENGTH OF INTERVIEW

$\overline{(1-4)}$ $\overset{010}{\overline{(6-8)}}$ $\overline{(13-18)}$ $\overline{(20-25)}$

SEQUENCE #   INTERVIEW ABSTRACT

— _____

— _____

— _____

— _____

— _____

— _____

— _____

— _____

— _____

— _____

— _____

— _____

— _____

— _____

— _____

— _____

— _____

— _____

— _____

— _____

— _____

$(10-11)$ $(13-77)$

ABSTRACTING FORM FOR ORAL HISTORY COMPUTER INDEX

INT. #   DATE   LENGTH OF INTERVIEW

(Sample of Completed Form)

0021 010   021776 83:20
(1-4) (6-8) (13-18) (20-25)

SEQUENCE #   INTERVIEW ABSTRACT

01 Mr. William B. Parker, Registrar, Business Manager (until 1945)

02 and Secretary to the Executive Faculty from 1925 to 1967

03 describes the formation of the Washington University School of

04 Medicine. Parker describes his previous jobs and his

05 appointment as Registrar, Business Manager and Secretary to

06 the Executive Faculty. He also describes the buildings, the

07 administrative offices and the duties of the Registrar in 1925

08 and some of the changes that occurred in later years. Parker

09 describes student recruitment trips and contrasts the students

10 and staff of 1925 with students and staff of 1976. He gives

11 the criteria of the Admissions Committee for selecting students

12 and describes the other Medical School Committees. Parker

13 lists the Deans, the Vice Chancellors for Medical Affairs, the

14 Assistant Registrars and the non-professional employees that

15 he worked with.

(10-11)   (13-77)

INDEXING FORM FOR ORAL HISTORY COMPUTER INDEX

INT. #   INTERVIEW NAME

 ___ 011b00 _____
(1-4) (6-11)   (13-43)

INT. #   SIDE & REEL #

 ___ 011 _____
(1-4) (6-8) (12-16)

MH	SEQ#	POSITION	INDEX TERMS

 ___   ___   _____   _____
(9)   (10-11)   (17-29)   (30-80)

INDEXING FORM FOR ORAL HISTORY COMPUTER INDEX

INT. #   INTERVIEW NAME

(Sample of Completed Form)

<u>0021</u> <u>011600</u> <u>William B. Parker</u>
(1-4) (6-11)   (13-43)

INT. #   SIDE & REEL #

<u>0021</u> <u>011</u> <u>20003</u>
(1-4) (6-8) (12-16)

MH	SEQ#	POSITION	INDEX TERMS
*	01	00:45-2:25	W.U.S.M. - History
	02		formation of, 1891-1909
*	01	2:30-2:55	Parker, William B.
	02		Appointed Registrar and Business Manager on
	03		August 1, 1925
*	01	3:00-3:40	Parker, William B.
	02		Graduate of the University of Missouri in 1921
*	01	3:45-4:30	Parker, William B.
	02		Employed by the University of Missouri
	03		throughout his college career
*	01	4:30-5:00	Parker, William B.
	02		Taught physical education and hygiene at West
	03		Port Junior High School in Kansas City, Missouri
	04		for two and one half years
*	01	5:00-5:10	Parker, William B.
	02		Assistant Registrar of the University of
	03		Missouri for one and one half years
*	01	5:40-7:20	Parker, William B.
	02		Business Manager of the Washington University
	03		School of Medicine until 1945
*	01	7:41-11:35	W.U.S.M. - History
	02		Buildings in 1925
(9)	(10-11)	(17-29)	(30-80)

Library Manual Appendix III, A-133

Subject: How to Make Corrections on the Oral History Computer Index.

1. The Oral History Computer Index is received from the Biomedical Computer Lab in two parts:

   a. An edit sheet which lists every card as it was read into the computer (See A-134).

   b. The actual index. The abstracts from all interviews are printed first, followed by an alphabetical list of the index terms for all interviews (See A-119 and A-120).

2. Examine the alphabetical index for errors such as misspellings, incorrect mainheadings, etc.

3. If errors are found, it is necessary to fill out another Indexing Form for Oral History Computer Index (See A-131) indicating the corrections. Write "Corrections" across the top of the form. Use a separate form for each interview, listing only the items that need correcting.

4. If a correction in one line will cause a change in the next line, it is necessary to also change the card for the second or subsequent lines.

5. Use the edit sheet to locate the cards that were keypunched incorrectly. Write the correction on the back of the card and replace it backwards in the deck. This makes it easier to locate the incorrect card when the correct card comes from keypunching.

6. If there is a mistake in the abstract, the corrections must be made on the Abstracting Form for Oral History Computer Index (See A-129) and labeled "Correction". Follow steps 3, 4 and 5.

7. Check the edit sheet of the printout for errors in time. To make corrections in time, fill out the index form for that interview and add the lines that are affected by the change. Follow steps 3, 4 and 5.

8. Send the corrections to keypunching.

9. When correct cards are returned from keypunching, use the edit sheet to locate the area of the deck with the correction. Pull the incorrect cards which are backwards in the deck, and replace them with the correct cards. The correct cards are placed face up in the deck.

10. When all errors are corrected, rerun the computer program.

This manual sheet supersedes all previous instruction sheets.

August 1, 1978

052472 99:35

```
OOI  OIO 001  LEE CADY, M.C., MEMBER OF THE WASHINGTON UNIVERSITY SCHOOL OF
OOI  OIO 002  MEDICINE'S CLASS OF 1926, RELATES HIS EXPERIENCES AS COMMANDER
OOI  OIO 003  OF GENERAL HOSPITAL 21 DURING WORLD WAR II. GENERAL HOSPITAL
OOI  OIO 004  21 WAS AFFILIATED WITH WASHINGTON UNIVERSITY AND MANY OF THE
OOI  OIO 005  DOCTORS AND NURSES HAD BEEN ON THE FACULTY OR STAFF OF THE
OOI  OIO 006  SCHOOL OF MEDICINE AND BARNES HOSPITAL BEFORE THE UNIT WAS
OOI  OIO 007  ACTIVATED AT THE START OF WORLD WAR II. GENERAL HOSPITAL 21
OOI  OIO 008  WAS STATIONED FIRST AT BOU HANIFA, ALGERIA, THEN AT TERMINI DI
OOI  OIO 009  AGNANO, ITALY, AND FINALLY AT DIRECOURT, FRANCE. THE UNIT
OOI  OIO 010  SERVED WITH DISTINCTION OPERATING AT ABOVE RATED CAPACITY AND
OOI  OIO 011  MANY OF THE UNIT'S OFFICERS AND ENLISTED MEN ALSO RECEIVED DECORATIONS FOR
OOI  OIO 012  MANY OFFICERS DISTINGUISHED SERVICE. THE UNIT WAS DEMOBILIZED AT THE END OF
OOI  OIO 013  WORLD WAR II AND THE MEMBERS OF THE UNIT RETURNED TO THEIR
OOI  OIO 014  CIVILIAN PURSUITS.
OOI  OIO 015  LEE CADY,

      102::000  CADY, LEE D., RETURNED TO THE WASHINGTON UNIVERSITY SCHOOL OF
      102::000  MEDICINE FOR THE 50TH ANNIVERSARY OF HIS
      102::000  GRADUATION IN THE CLASS OF 1926
      102::000  W.U. CADY, LEE D., CLASS OF 1926
      129::55   CADY, GENERAL HOSPITAL 21
      129::55   CADY, LEE D.
      129::55   CADY, GENERAL HOSPITAL 21
      129::55   WORLD WAR II, GENERAL HOSPITAL 21
      129::55   CADY, GENERAL HOSPITAL 21
      129::25   WORLD WAR 1
      102::15   BASE HOSPITAL 21
      102::15   WORLD WAR 1
      102::35   GENERAL HOSPITAL 21, U.S. ARMY RESERVE
      102::35   CLOPTON, MALVERN B., COMMANDER
      102::35   CLOPTON, COMMANDER OF U.S. ARMY RESERVE, GENERAL
      102::35   HOSPITAL 21
      102::30   U.S. ARMY RESERVE, GENERAL HOSPITAL 21
      102::50   CADY, CLOPTON, MALVERN B., COMMANDER
      103::15   KERR, 2ND LIEUTENANT IN THE INFANTRY
      103::10   KERR, ROBERT, PROFESSOR OF MILITARY SCIENCE AND TACTICS
      104::10   CADY, EXECUTIVE OFFICER OF U.S. ARMY RESERVE.
      104::10   GENERAL HOSPITAL 21, U.S. ARMY RESERVE
      104::10   CADY, LEE D., EXECUTIVE OFFICER
      104::40   U.S. ARMY RESERVE, GENERAL HOSPITAL 21
      104::15   CADY, LEE D., EXECUTIVE OFFICER
      106::05   CADY, TWO TRIPS TO WASHINGTON, D.C. REGARDING U.S.
      106::15   ARMY RESERVE, GENERAL HOSPITAL 21
      106::15   CADY, LEE D., TWO TRIPS TO WASHINGTON, D.C. REGARDING U.S.
      104::40   ARMY RESERVE, GENERAL HOSPITAL 21
```